CM00741206

The Toad

and

The Jaguar

The Toad

and

The Jaguar

A Field Report of Underground Research
on a Visionary Medicine

Bufo alvarius and *5-methoxy-dimethyltryptamine*

by
Ralph Metzner

With Forewords by
Stanislav Grof, MD, and Charles Grob, MD

Green Earth Foundation
&
Regent Press

ISBN-13: 978-1-58790-254-3
ISBN-10: 1-58790-254-0
Library of Congress Control Number: 2013951986

Cover Photos
Sonora Desert toad (Bufo alvarius)
Wooden alebrije jaguar mask from Oaxaca, Mexico

Layout and Design
Cynthia Smith

Published by
REGENT PRESS
www.regentpress.net

for

GREEN EARTH FOUNDATION
www.greenearthfound.org

Printed in the U.S.A.
REGENT PRESS
2747 Regent Street
Berkeley, CA 94705
e-mail: regentpress@mindspring.com

Printed on recycled paper

Nothing in this book should be construed as my advocacy of the use of the drugs or substances described herein. Nor do I advocate the breaking of any state or federal laws relating to the use of these or any other drugs.

Contents

The difference between the remedy and the poison — is the dosage.

Theophrastus Paracelsus
16th century

The highest stage of seeing is achieved when the border-line between subject and object, between observer and observed, between myself and the external world, is consciously lifted and I am unified with the world and its spiritual primal source. That is the condition of love.

Albert Hofmann
20th century

Foreword by
Charles S. Grob, MD

Over the last half century remarkable discoveries have been made of the capacity of particular chemical compounds to induce profoundly altered states of consciousness. One of the pioneers of this revolutionary science has been Ralph Metzner, who began his career in 1960 at Harvard University. At the forefront of our evolving understanding of the potential for psychedelics to facilitate healing and spiritual awareness, Metzner was one of the first to identify the critical importance of set and setting to ensure optimal outcome, and in particular the physical and psychological safety of those who have chosen to explore these mysteries of the inner realms. While early in his career he was an acknowledged scientific expert on the range of effects of synthesized psychedelic compounds, in more recent years he has avidly explored the relationship of the human species to the natural world, focusing on the remarkable range of visionary plants long known to the indigenous people of the earth, and only recently "discovered" by modernity.

The Toad and the Jaguar is Metzner's latest contribution to our understanding of such consciousness altering compounds, with the introduction of his impressive studies of the powerful and until recently poorly understood neurochemical compound, 5-methoxy DMT (5-methoxy dimethyltryptamine), and its manifestation in nature in both plant form indigenous to the Amazon rainforest and most curiously, contained in the glandular secretions of a particular species of toad whose habitat is the vast desert bordering Mexico and the south-west United States.

It is remarkable that the human central nervous system possesses such exquisite sensitivity to the effects of psychedelics. With the prototype synthetic hallucinogen, lysergic acid diethyamide (LSD), receptivity is on the order of micrograms, an astonishingly miniscule quantity. With other psychedelic compounds, including psilocybin, mescaline and the tryptamines, while they do not possess such micro dose potency, their effects nevertheless induce profoundly altered states of consciousness that open the potential for life transformative experiences. Valued as sacraments of the highest order by the native peoples, their emergence into the turmoil and challenge of modern civilization demand that they be regarded with the greatest respect. We may also pause to reflect on the ontological significance of the human central nervous system, evolving from the earliest life forms on the planet to develop such remarkable and exquisite receptivity to so highly unusual a class of psychoactive compounds. It has become clear that the human brain has in a sense been programed to respond to these plants of the Gods, as the great pioneers Schultes and Hofmann would put it. It is up to us, the inheritors of all the traditions and peoples that have passed from the earth, to make sense and learn how to optimally utilize these divine gifts.

Beyond examining the powerful mind altering and potentially positive life changing impact of 5-methoxy DMT, Metzner provides a valuable service by also examining the dark side of the potential for misuse and abuse, where vulnerable users taking the compound under adverse conditions are at risk for injury. It is imperative that we learn how to implement optimal models for administering such powerful compounds as 5-methoxy DMT. Examination of traditional sacramental use emphasizes the importance of set and setting, as well as the expertise and ethical integrity of the facilitator. After a several decade freeze of formal investigations of hallucinogens, opportunities have recently opened to resume formal sanctioned studies of their effects in human users, both normal volunteers as well as subjects with clinical disorders that have not responded to conventional treatments. The time has arrived where we are once again able to resume these valuable explorations that were prematurely ended owing to the relative cultural immaturity existing during the 1960s. The question now before us is whether we as a society have sufficiently evolved so that we are able to contain and support investigations of this vital yet long-neglected field.

Necessary foundational work still needs to be done to determine the range of physiological and psychological effects of 5-methoxy DMT, ensuring that accurate safety parameters are fully understood for such phenomena as blood pressure regulation as well as mental stability. Through his own experimentation, Metzner has already identified that administration through nasal insufflation may be significantly safer than consuming the drug in either smoked, vaporized or especially injected form. He also suggests that a range of psychiatric, psychosomatic and even immunologic disorders might possibly be amenable to a treatment model employing such compounds.

It will be essential that care is taken to employ a knowledgeable, respectful and ethical approach to this work, and avoid triggering the antagonistic cultural reactions that occurred following the sudden introduction of psychedelics into society during the 1960s. Great potential exists for the rigorous study of psychedelics to reveal new and more effective treatments for people suffering from intractable and nonresponsive conditions, as well as instruct us in new ways of relating to the Earth so we may address the growing concerns over environmental degradation and climatic change. It is imperative, however, that we fully learn from the lessons of the past, and avoid the pitfalls that doomed the promising early investigations in the field.

We owe a debt of gratitude for the vital work these early explorers in the field of psychedelic research have contributed to our world. Ralph Metzner himself has spanned the generations, a leading scholar and investigator during the early, halcyon days of psychedelic discovery and a steady persistent presence over the successive decades of repression and now reopening of this long dormant field. His courageous and unflagging efforts have kept the vision alive, and continue to provide new insights and new paths for further evolution of our understanding of this vital and fascinating field of study. *The Toad and the Jaguar* is but the latest contributions of a career that has helped to open our eyes to the profound mysteries and transformative potentials that nature offers us through her sacred plants and chemicals.

Charles S. Grob, MD

Director of the Division of Child and Adolescent Psychiatry at Harbor-UCLA Medical Center, and Professor of Psychiatry and Pediatrics at the UCLA School of Medicine. He is also a founding board member of the Heffter Research Institute.

Foreword by
Stanislav Grof, MD, PhD

The two decades following Albert Hofmann's serendipitous discovery of the psychedelic effects of LSD-25 have been called the "golden era of psychopharmacology." The discovery of new psychedelics and a renaissance of interest in those already known brought into psychiatry new hope – the promise of therapy that could address the causes of emotional disorders rather than just suppress the symptoms. At the same time laboratory research of psychedelics generated revolutionary new information about neuroreceptors, neurotransmitters, and drug interactions in the brain.

After the unfortunate and misdirected administrative and legal overreaction to unsupervised mass use of psychedelics in the 1960s, all scientific research in this promising area was effectively stopped. It took the academic community forty years to recognize that the potential of psychedelic substances deserves to be seriously examined. During this period some fascinating psychedelics could not have been synthesized, discovered, and explored had it not been for dedicated individuals and groups convinced about the scientific, psychological, and spiritual potential of psychedelics and entheogens. They carried on informal exploration of these medicines and sacraments without official permission, taking advantage of legal loopholes and the slow pace of the criminalization of new substances.

These enthusiastic explorers have amassed large amount of invaluable information that could in the future serve as a basis for well designed and organized research projects. During the last thirty years Ralph Metzner, an experienced researcher and pioneer of psychedelic research, kept contact with these groups in USA and in Europe and collected data about their experiences with entheogenic tryptamine derivatives that he is now making available in his ground-breaking book *The Toad and the Jaguar*. The main focus of the book is on a substance that seems particularly fascinating and promising, *5-methoxy-DMT*, a psychoactive alkaloid extracted from South American indigenous snuff powders and the venom of the toad *Bufo alvarius*.

The book provides detailed information concerning the phenomenology of the experience, therapeutic effects, modes of administration, the dose-effect relationship, impact of various settings, combination of entheogenic sessions with various forms of spiritual practice, and comparison of *5-methoxy-DMT* with its cousins *DMT* and *bufotenine*. Particularly interesting seems to be the potential of *5-methoxy-DMT* as a future therapeutic agent because it is sufficiently powerful to induce therapeutic and transformative effects within a time period that does not put unreasonable demands on the therapists' schedule and thereby makes it easier to contain the experience.

The Toad and the Jaguar is an extraordinary contribution to psychedelic literature that will in the future be seen as a classic. The information that it brings is sufficiently convincing to inspire clinical research on *5-methoxy-DMT*. What immediately comes to mind is a study that would test the effects of this substance in the treatment of PTSD in veterans and might have the best chance to be approved because of the enormity of the problems with this diagnostic category.

Research of *5-methoxy-DMT* should also be of great interest for psychoneuropharmacologists, because *tryptamine* is a derivative of the amino acid *tryptophan* and occurs naturally in the human body. This research might provide insights into the mechanisms associated with spontaneously occurring episodes of non-ordinary states of consciousness and mystical experiences.

Stanislav Grof, MD, PhD
Founding president of the International Transpersonal Association, author of *LSD Psychotherapy, Psychology of the Future, Healing Our Deepest Wounds* and other works.

The Toad and the Jaguar

A Field Report of Underground Research on a Visionary Medicine

5-Meo-DMT *(5-methoxy-dimethyltryptamine)* only became listed as a Schedule I controlled substance in Jan 2011, whereas its better-known chemical relative *DMT* has been scheduled and banned since the mid-1960s. As a result, the psychopharmacological and entheogenic explorations related here, which took place at various times during the past thirty years, have been conducted entirely legally. My esteemed colleague and friend, the Chilean psychiatrist Claudio Naranjo, who collaborated in some of the early experimental trials of new substances with Alexander Shulgin, once told me that it was a conscious choice on their part not to mention this substance in their published writings, so it would pass under the censorious radar of the prohibitionists. I have myself kept to this implicit secrecy commitment in my previous writings; but now that the "cat is out of the bag," so to speak, and the substance has attained the perverse recognition of prohibition, I feel that the time is ripe for truth-telling.

In this monograph, I relate my findings from more than 30 years of experiences and observations with this substance in various user groups and individuals, both in the US and in Europe. It is the prelude to a subsequent volume in which I will record my observations concerning the other major hallucinogenic/

psychedelic substances. I use the term "underground" in referring to the explorations with these substances, in the sense that they were hidden, out of respect for the restrictions and prohibitions of mainstream culture. I do not regard this culture as counter to or opposed to mainstream political systems. Rather, as far as I can tell, interest in "mind-assisting plants" (to use Thomas Berry's felicitous phrase) seems to be congruent with a wide spectrum of diverse political and religious orientations.

5-Meo-DMT is found naturally, along with its better known (and long illegal) chemical relative DMT, as well as other indole alkaloids, in snuff preparations variously called *epena* or *paricá*, made from the bark resin of several species of Virola trees (particularly *V. theiodora*). These Virola snuffs are used by the Tukano, Waika, Yanomama and other Indians of the western Amazon and Orinoco basin, who refer to it as "semen of the sun." It produces an out-of-body, dissociated state, which shamans use ritualistically to connect with positive, life-supporting spirits for healing and divination, and for defensive actions against hostile spirits (Schultes, R.E. & Hofmann, A., 1979).

There is anthropological, as well as archaeological, evidence for another powerful shamanic snuff preparation variously called *yopo, vilca* or *cebil,* derived from the powdered seed/beans of several species of *Anadenanthera* tree (*A. colubrina* and *A. peregrina*). These snuff preparations were also used in the Amazon and in northern Argentina; and the seeds apparently traded with cultures in the Atacama desert of Northern Argentina, where snuffing paraphernalia with seed pods have been found dating back to the second millennium BCE (Torres, C.M. & Repke, D.B., 2006). The chemical constituent of the *Anadenanthera* snuffs is primarily *bufotenine* (5-hydroxy-dimethyltryptamine), which has uncertain psychoactive properties that have only recently begun to be documented and researched. In the following monograph, I will not be discussing *bufotenine*, since my own (limited) personal exploration with it suggests to me that, despite the close similarity in chemical structure, it has nothing close to the profound psychoactivity of *5-methoxy-DMT*.

Bufotenine, as it's name suggests (*bufo* = Latin "toad"), is also found in the secretions of some species of toad and has, like *DMT*, been listed on Schedule I since the 1960s. A shamanic use of toad venom has not been documented in the ethnological literature, although it is inferred from the extensive presence of toad imagery in Maya iconography of the classical period. In a 1992 paper on the "Identity of a New World Psychoactive Toad," Wade Davis and Andrew Weil rejected the previously proposed identification of *Bufo marinus* as the candidate species because of the toxicity of its venom (Davis, W. & Weil, A. 1992).

They proposed instead the Sonora desert toad, *Bufo alvarius*, which "though known to be toxic when consumed orally, may be safely smoked and is powerfully psychoactive by that route of administration...providing clear evidence of a psychoactive toad that could have been employed by Precolumbian peoples of the New World" (*op. cit.* p. 51). The primary psychoactive constituent of *Bufo alvarius* venom is not *bufotenine*, but 5-Meo-DMT. Davis and Weil concluded that smoking selectively denatures the toxic constituents in the raw venom. They add that "one *B. alvarius* toad yields 0.25 to 0.5gm of dried venom. Since concentrations of 5-Meo-DMT may be as high as 15%, one toad may yield 75 mg of a hallucinogenic drug that, when smoked, is effective in humans at doses of 3-5 mg. In other words, a single toad produces 12-25 doses of one of the most psychoactive drugs in nature" (*op. cit.* p. 57).

I emphasize that what I am reporting in this monograph are not experiments with placebo control groups, as is customary in the scientific testing of new and unknown drugs. With these substances (variously called *psychedelic, hallucinogenic* or *entheogenic*), medical science is not yet at the stage where they are about to be introduced into the psychiatric-pharmaceutical market place. (A possible exception is the synthetic MDMA, which may soon, hopefully, be approved as an adjunct for the psychotherapeutic treatment of PTSD). Rather, what we have are ethnographic field reports: first-hand observations from an underground sub-culture, accompanied by the experience reports of a number of participant-observers. My suggestions of possible cerebral processes triggered by these substances are of course hypothetical and would need to be subjected to the customary tests and replications of scientific methodology.

At the same time, I emphasize that in research with these and other so-called psychedelic or entheogenic substances, one cannot limit the observations and reflections solely to their physical and psychological effects. As most of the people cited here emphasize, the experiences they've had with these substances at times go far beyond the physical and psychological into the deepest and highest dimensions, both the cosmic and the spiritual – and even into the divine realms spoken of by the mystics of all traditions. These are experiential realms where descriptive words and images of necessity give way to indescribable awe and wonder.

Experiences with smoking Bufo alvarius *toad venom*

Wade Davis, in the above mentioned paper, describes his own trial with inhalation of dried *B. alvarius* venom as follows:

Shortly after inhalation, I experienced warm flushing sensations, a sense of wonder and well-being, strong auditory hallucinations, which included an insect-cicada sound that ran across my mind and seemed to link my body to the earth. Though I was indoors, there was a sense of the feel of the earth, the dry desert soil passing through my fingers, the stars at midday, the scent of cactus and sage, the feel of dry leaves through hands. Strong visual hallucinations in orblike brilliance, diamond patterns that undulated across my visual field (Davis, W. and Weil, A., *op. cit.* p. 56).

A friend of mine has reported that in his experiences with ayahuasca (which contains both DMT and 5-Meo-DMT) he also has heard this kind of cicada-like sound. For the brothers Terence and Dennis McKenna, in the ayahuasca and mushroom trips they related in their autobiographical *The Invisible Landscape*, hearing and then autonomously reproducing the interior sound vibration they heard during the journey, seemed to precipitate a quantum jump to another dimension of reality (McKenna, T. & McKenna, D., 1975).

In the interests of maintaining an honorable ethical stance toward another member of the animal kingdom, I should state here that it is entirely possible and, one could say, obligatory, that the extraction of the exudate of a toad, like *B. alvarius* or any other, can be and should be safely and effectively carried out without any harm to the individual toad.

In the late 1980s, having already had some powerful and revelatory experiences (to be described below) with smoking synthetic 5-Meo-DMT, I decided to join with two experienced friends in an expedition to harvest the venom of *Bufo alvarius* for further trials. So it came about that I found myself in the outskirts of Tucson, Arizona during the rainy season, to harvest some of the hallucinogenic exudate of the Colorado River toad. This magnificent amphibian lives now actually mostly in the Sonora Desert (hence its other name), spending nine months of the year buried up to two feet down in the moist underground of Mother Earth. They emerge after the rains, which are often very sparse, for an orgy of feeding and copulation, hanging out in grassy terrain near waterways, hopping around under street lights at night to catch flying insects, which is where we found them. Unlike their long-legged cousins the frogs, toads can't really jump – they just sort of hop around, and are easy to catch.

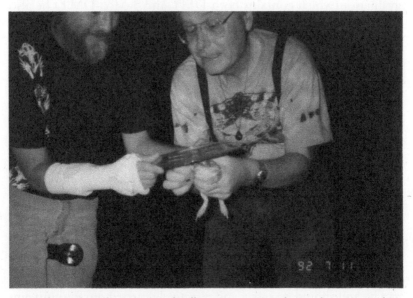

Author (somewhat tense) and colleague extracting the psychoactive toad venom from specimens of *Bufo alvarius* for use as research materials.

Some of the larger specimens barely fit onto a grown man's hand, measuring maybe six inches from head to rear and four inches in width; plus they seem to be able to expand their girth, puffing up to make themselves even fatter. The weight and feel of them is like that of a small plucked chicken – except that the body is very soft and yielding, and you don't really feel any bones. The skin is olive-green in hue, with little bumpy warts, two large raised parotid glands, 1/2 inch in length, at the neck, and smaller glands at the crook of the elbows and groins. We worked in pairs: one of us would pick up a toad, holding it gently but firmly from the top with one hand, and then squeezing the gland with thumb and forefinger of the other hand so that the milky white slime would squirt or ooze out onto a sheet of plastic or glass held by the other man. The exudate sticks to the glass and is left to dry overnight. It can then be scraped off with a razor blade, in the form of little flakes and crumbs, which can then be put in a pipe or vaporizer and smoked.

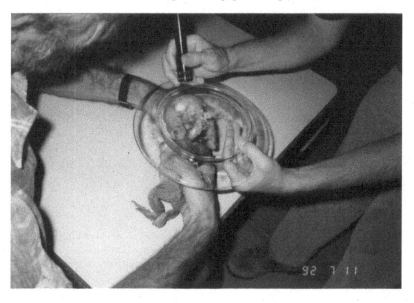

My personal attitude towards toads, carried over from childhood ignorance and rumor, had been a mixture of aversion and fear. I had somehow acquired the mistaken belief that they could squirt poison at you. But by the time of this expedition my attitude had changed to admiring, even reverential. I had already had the opportunity to experience the effects of the psychoactive ingredient of the venom of this particular toad, which is also present in several South American entheogenic snuff preparations, as mentioned above. My experiences with this substance, a chemical relative of DMT, have been among the most profound transcendent and healing experiences of my life, although they have also included challenging and frightening times. So any negative subjective feelings about toads were outweighed by the memory awareness of previous enlightening experiences with synthetic 5-Meo-DMT and the knowledge that it could be safely ingested in this form.

You might say I was prepared to worship the Toad Deity that could induce such magical experiences in humans. We approached the lovely creatures with admiration and respect. When I lifted one up I would talk to it softly. I remember being amazed at their soft, weighty body, with its skin not slimy at all, and the most beautiful jet-black round eyes, shining like black pearls. We murmured prayers of gratitude and assurances that we would not hurt them. We told them how the medicine they produced would help us humans understand the nature of reality and give us cosmic healing visions. After milking the exudate, we replaced them gently on the ground. We had been informed that the toad can replenish its store of venom in about two weeks and is otherwise not harmed.

The venom serves the toad for defense: a dog or coyote attempting to bite it would get a shot of the hallucinogenic slime into the mouth or eyes, which would not kill but definitely distract the predator from its purpose. We talked to a woman in Tucson who had several dogs and lots of the toads hanging around her pool. One of her dogs had evidently assaulted a toad, and she found him lolling around on the ground on his back, tongue hanging out and drooling, eyes rolling wildly. After twenty minutes the dog got up and walked away apparently unharmed, its predatory interest in the toad forgotten.

On another occasion, the family dog in a friend's house had somehow found and ingested a sizable portion of the powdered toad slime that was lying in a package on a low table, while the owner and fellow psychonauts, including myself, were sitting and conversing in an adjacent room. Not knowing what the dog had done, we became alarmed when we saw the dog lying stretched out on the ground, motionless except for shallow breathing. We rushed him by car to the nearest vet, a trip that took about 20 minutes, and by the time we got there he was almost back to his tail-wagging happy self.

There are varying amounts of other ingredients in the toad slime, such as *bufotenine*, which may be more toxic. It is believed the toxins are active when absorbed directly through mucous membranes (of mouth, nostrils or eyes), but are inactivated by the heat of smoking. Later in this essay, I will describe our experiments with the ingestion of synthesized pure 5-Meo-DMT by nasal insufflation – the snuffing method. For the synthesized pure substance this is physiologically completely safe, whereas for the toad venom, with its mixture of ingredients, the snuff method could potentially be toxic, or at least unpleasant.

My two companions and I returned home from our expedition with a supply of the dried toad venom, which we proceeded to test out with self-experiments. Bret B. recorded the following observations from his trial.

> I think the smoking technique is very important and a bit hard to learn – you want to maximize vaporizing the dried venom into an opaque white smoke, while minimizing carbonizing the material with direct flame contact. In my experience, this can have the most overwhelming, positively life-changing effect, when done in the right circumstances. Once this summer, in

the mountains at 12,000 feet, there was an approaching thunderstorm, and during the peak of my experience, where there was no internal dialogue, ego having been dissolved, I felt an intimate contact with the lightning storm. At that point, it was raining all around us, but not on us. I sat up, opened my eyes and looked straight up into the clouds, and it was even more intense than with eyes closed. Some part of me was in a dialogue with the lightning. I would frame a question, something like "are you there?" and get an immediate lightning bolt nearby as an answer.

I used to have bad rheumatoid arthritis. I felt my spine trying to move, and a wave motion began at its base up to my head, and I felt something go shooting straight up to the clouds directly above me, and this was answered in about a millisecond by a terrifically loud lightning bolt very nearby. All pain of all kinds disappeared immediately in my body – joint, muscular, backaches, everything, and no pain of any even minor normal body kind returned for 48 hours. As I was coming out of the experience, I felt a strong sense of the long span of evolution of life on the planet, and an awareness of other, larger, perhaps eon-spanning entities that in states like this can become aware of us. In this context I felt that we humans were like microbes to them.

I can add that the healing and pain-reducing effect of the toad venom, and of its synthetic equivalent (5-Meo-DMT), has been confirmed by others, myself included, several times – and this is a topic that deserves further investigation. My speculative hypothesis is that the medicine appears to induce a profound state of relaxation and painless fluidity at the neuro-muscular junctions – which, though temporary, can leave one with a hopeful long-term, memory-based positive outlook toward healing. Charles Grob, MD (personal communication) has suggested that, if these observations are confirmed, there could be some role for this substance in treating neuro-muscular diseases like myasthenia gravis, where the current state of the art treatment involves large doses of corticosteroids, which have serious adverse side effects.

The pure substance is active in the dose range of 5–15 mg. Each exudate of an adult toad may contain as much as 75 mg. That means each toad is loaded with enough energetic force to launch seven to ten adult human beings potentially into cosmic hyper-consciousness, to the heart of creation, and return them safely to their human form. This is the mystery then: why and how does the toad do that, or have that power? Why is its defense survival reaction such that humans, who don't really even prey on toads, can experience mystical transcendence from it? At the least, it is evidence for the interconnected web of all life at the molecular level. All life on Earth does use the same DNA molecule as the code of procreation and genetic transmission.

A passage from Shakespeare's *As You Like It* seems to be associating a secret knowledge of this all-embracing consciousness, a mystical oneness with nature, with the ancient tradition of a toad with jewels in its head. The image seems strangely significant, in view of the multitudes of glittering jewels one can sometimes see when ingesting the venom of this particular toad (or its synthetic equivalent).

> Sweet are the uses of adversity,
> Which, like the toad, ugly and venomous,
> Wears yet a precious jewel in his head.
> And this our life, exempt from public haunt,
> Finds tongues in trees, books in running brooks,
> Sermons in stones and good in everything.

Effective and dissociative dosage levels

In comparison with DMT, the use of which has been extensively studied and documented both in scientific research (especially through the work of Rick Strassman, MD) and in the underground internet literature, information on 5-Meo-DMT dosage levels is sparse. As I suggested at the beginning of this essay there may be a particular historical reason for the paucity of research with this substance.

In animal pharmacology research, it is customary to measure or estimate a minimally effective dose (ED-50) of a given substance, the level at which a response can be observed in 50% of the subjects; and a lethal dose (LD-50), the level at which 50% of the experimental animals die. The equivalent human toxic levels of that drug are then estimated by extrapolation, in relation to body weight. In the underground culture of psychoactive substance use, the danger of excessive dosages is not physiological collapse or death (as long as the drugs used are free of impurities), but psychological *dissociation*: unconsciousness of one's own bodily postures and gestures, vocalizations and verbalizations, as well as more or less total disconnect of awareness of one's surroundings.

In my book *MindSpace and TimeStream*, I pointed out that although psychedelic states are typically characterized by a vast increase in mental and visual associations, i.e. expansions of consciousness, dissociative and contracted states may occur with psychedelics if the dosage is too high for that individual, so that the amplified sensations and perceptions cannot be assimilated. "It is important to realize that dissociated drug states, involving a profound disconnect from time-space reality, are quite different than the classic psychosis-like 'bad trip' marked by confusion, high anxiety, strange sensations and distorted perceptions" (Metzner, R. *op. cit.* p.105).

Dissociative experiences are those which cannot be meaningfully remembered or described – the person may simply notice afterwards that some time has elapsed and their memory is blank. Such dissociated experiences (or episodes within an experience) may not be accompanied by feelings of anxiety, and may not be reported as "bad trips" by the person. There may be no feelings at all, or the person may report feeling calm or even blissful. Other observers may report the person uttering strange verbalizations or vocalizations and assuming unusual bodily positions or movements, of which the subject has no memory whatsoever. Such postural and vocal dissociative reactions can be alarming to others, though the persons themselves may report no discomfort or distress at the time, or afterwards.

Here are some examples of dissociative experiences extracted from the accounts of 5-Meo-DMT trials in Shulgin's *TIHKAL – The Continuation.*

> I was not there in my body or in time..my mind was completely referenceless…An inability to judge in any way, by any method of the mind (with 15 mg, smoked).

> There was no distance, no possibility of examining the experience…I have very little memory of the state itself, no memory of whether my eyes were open or closed (with 25 mg, smoked).

> An instant later (after 30 mg smoked) I was crawled up on my bed, in the fetal position, with my eyes closed, squirming around, screaming in my head, "Fuck! You killed yourself." I repeated this several times, very fearful of death. I didn't see anything…I concentrated on breathing and that helped me survive (mentally). Next memory was of putting a CD on the stereo – to my surprise 40 minutes had passed, in what I remembered as mere seconds (Shulgin, A. & A., 1997, pp. 533-534).

The Shulgins, in their compendium on psychoactive trypt-amines, give 6–20 mg as the "general dosage range" for 5-Meo-DMT ingestion by smoking or vapor inhalation. For comparison, the general effective dosage they give for smoking DMT is 60-100 mg. Similar dosage ranges are also given in *Psychedelische Chemie* by Daniel Trachsel (2000). This means that 5-Meo-DMT is 8-10 times as potent as the simpler molecule DMT, though both can reach the same intensity and depth of experience, i.e. are equally powerful.[1] They do not provide data on ingestion by snuffing the purified synthetic powder.

I suggest that the two important dosage figures to estimate and communicate, for human participant-observer research with this and other psychoactive substances, are:

ED-50: the threshold dosage at which psychoactive effects are observed by about half the subjects, or in half the trials; and

DD-50: the dosage at which about half the subjects, or half the experiences, involve some degree of dissociation.

From the published data in the Shulgins' *TIHKAL* and on the internet, and from my own observations in underground research circles, I would estimate the ED-50 of smoked or inhaled 5-Meo-DMT to be 5 mg and the DD-50 15 mg. The comparison figures for DMT (from Shulgin and my own observations) are 50-60 mg for the ED-50 and 100-150 mg for the DD-50.

These figures correspond with the dosage estimates (in the paper cited above by Wade Davis and Andrew Weil) for *Bufo alvarius* venom, and indicate that 5-Meo-DMT is about 10 times

---

[1] In pharmacology, the power of a drug is the intensity of the observed response; whereas the potency is the inverse of the amount needed to produce a given response. For example, LSD and mescaline are equally powerful, i.e. can produce an equally intense experience; but LSD is a thousand times more potent – 100 micrograms of LSD are equivalent in power to 100 milligrams of mescaline.

the potency of the simpler molecule DMT. This confirms the common observation that it takes 3 or 4 inhalations to smoke DMT to an effective dosage level, whereas an effective dose of 5-Meo-DMT can be inhaled in one breath. These dosage ranges are also confirmed by the dissociative reactions quoted above, from *TIHKAL*, which involved doses of 15 mg or higher for 5-Meo-DMT.

Individual factors affecting intensity of experience

Besides the effective and dissociative dosage levels, there are three additional factors that can affect an individual's response to this as well as to other psychoactive substances: body weight, innate sensitivity and prior experience or learning. *Body weight*. In medical pharmacology, dosage levels are customarily given in terms of mg per kg of body weight. The effective and dissociative dosages for a lighter person will be lower than those for a heavier person.

Innate sensitivity. There are inherent or innate differences in nervous system perceptual sensitivity – that are not easily recognized or measurable by any presently known medical or psychological instrumentation. At the high end of the sensitivity spectrum there are individuals, sometimes called clairvoyant or clairsentient, who respond more strongly and vividly than average to any perceptual stimuli, whether external or internal. Many artists and so-called psychics or intuitives fall in this category. The intensity of their perceptual and affective response to a given stimulus is stronger than average. Therefore the effective and dissociative dosage for them would tend to be lower than average.

This factor of innate individual differences in response sensitivity is not generally appreciated in the underground drug subculture, according to my observations. A given dose of a drug can produce effects differing in intensity in different individuals – even when the other factors of set and setting are held constant. I believe such unrecognized individual differences in response sensitivity is an additional factor that can lead to unpleasant and non-useful dissociative experiences in those who are focussed solely on the specifics of the drugs ingested.

Experiential learning. In the groups I've observed, people seemed to learn through experience what their inherent sensitivity is and adjust their intake accordingly. Experienced inner space explorers and those who devote careful attention to the set and setting of their explorations will be far less likely to have dissociative elements in their experience than inexperienced and ill-prepared "trippers." The range between the ED-50 and the DD-50 can be considered the level at which the average intelligent, well-informed, seeker-observer can expect to have philosophically meaningful and/or psychologically useful experiences.

Mode of ingestion and duration of effect

An important practical comparison between the two substances (DMT and 5-Meo-DMT) is in the mode of ingestion and the duration of effect. Both substances have an almost immediate onset when smoked or vaporized, because the smoke is absorbed through the mucous membranes of the mouth and throat, as well as the lungs. DMT is very rapidly metabolized, the effect extinguishing in about 3-5 minutes with an apparent rapid decline of concentrations in cerebral circulation. The effect of 5-Meo-DMT also starts almost immediately upon inhalation, though it is apparently metabolized more slowly, since the effect lasts about 15-20 minutes, i.e. three times as long as DMT. Thus with the smoking or vaporizer inhalation method of ingestion, 5-Meo-DMT affords a longer time period for shamanic or therapeutic practice and application.

The lower effective dosage and longer time duration of 5-Meo-DMT, as compared to DMT, is a distinct advantage in view of the somewhat complicated procedure required for inhalation. Whereas a person smoking DMT may need to take 3-4 full inhalations to get to an effective intensity level, an effective amount of 5-Meo-DMT can usually be inhaled in one inbreath. This is exemplified in the account by Stanislav Grof, cited below, in which he reports that he sat still as a stone, in deep absorptive trance after one inhalation from the pipe, which others then removed from his hands.

The extremely short duration of the effects of both these tryptamines, due to their being rapidly metabolized, is also a pharmacological safety feature. Whether the experience is ecstatic or traumatic, in 99% of cases there is a return to normal body-centered ego-consciousness within 5-15 minutes – particularly if the session is taking place in a protected and familiar setting.

This is not true of drugs like LSD, psilocybin or ayahuasca, in which, as is well-known, painful and confusing "bad trips," sometimes with complex paranoid scenarios, can go on for hours or even (rarely) for days. The short duration of the neurological intoxication was exemplified in the experiences of the dogs related above, who returned to their usual happy canine behavior within about 30 minutes, despite having accidentally ingested a hefty dose of 5-Meo-DMT in toad venom.

Cosmic consciousness, transcendence and dissociation

The distinction between dissociation and transcendence is not always easy to make, even for individuals with experiential background in Eastern or Western spiritual teachings. In the course of the Harvard project in the early 1960s, we experimented with DMT in the form of intra-muscular injections. While most of us found the experience to be more or less out-of-body, chaotic and dissociative, one of our visitors was an Indian with extensive experience in kundalini yoga, who after the injection assumed a seated yoga posture, closed his eyes and sat motionless and silent in deep meditative absorption for 40 minutes, thanked us and left.

Someone with little or no prior experience with meditative states or practices might simply go completely unconscious, i.e. dissociate, while those with more experience might find themselves in transcendent, out-of-body or absorptive trance states that can be only partially remembered and described afterwards. Body movements, sounds and verbal utterances that are observed by others but not remembered by the subject, indicate dissociative disconnect, no matter how pleasurable the subjective experience. The ability to make sense of the experience would certainly be a function of having had some prior experiences of transcendent consciousness and acquaintance with the literature of meditative practices.

Stanislav Grof, a very experienced explorer of psychedelic realities, relates an experience with 5-Meo-DMT in his autobiographical book *When the Impossible Happens* (Grof, S. 2006). He smoked what he later estimated to have been 25 mg, i.e. at the high end of the dosage spectrum, unaware of the extreme potency of this substance. He describes dissociative aspects early in the experience:

I lost all contact with the surrounding world, which completely disappeared...The awareness of my everyday existence, my name, my whereabouts and my life disappeared... I tried hard to remind myself of the existence of the realities I used to know, but they suddenly did not make any sense... There was no biographical or transpersonal content, images, archetypes...none of these dimensions seemed to exist, let alone manifest. I had no concepts, no categories for what I was witnessing.

A little bit later he started to name his experience in terms of Tibetan Buddhist after-death teachings, of which he had made extensive study – believing that his physical body had actually died.

My only reality was a mass of radiant swirling energy of immense proportions that seemed to contain all existence in a condensed and entirely abstract form. I became Consciousness facing the Absolute. It had the brightness of myriad suns, yet it was not on the same continuum with any light I knew from everyday life. It seemed to be pure consciousness, intelligence, and creative energy transcending all polarities. It was infinite and finite, divine and demonic, terrifying and ecstatic, creative and destructive...My ordinary identity was shattered and dissolved; I became one with the Source. I retrospect, I believe I must have experienced the *Dharmakaya*, the Primary Clear Light, which according to the *Tibetan Book of the Dead*, appears at the moment of our death.

...Some timeless time later, dreamlike images began to emerge, the solar system, the Earth...the last to emerge was the sense of my everyday identity and awareness of my present life. I was sure that I had taken a dose that was excessive and that I was actually dying... I believed I was experiencing the bardo, the intermediate state before my rebirth in the next incarnation. Then I was seeing and experiencing many scenes from my past lives, playing out karmic history in my body but at the same time in a state of profound bliss, completely detached from these dramas(Grof, S. *op. cit.*, pp. 251-257).

My own experiences with 5-Meo-DMT also began with the smoking of an unspecified (though clearly large) amount brought by a colleague to the Esalen Institute, where I was visiting. I was surrounded by compassionate friends and felt completely safe and protected – though also totally unprepared for what followed.

> A shattering annihilation, a feeling of being inside an explosion, and being fragmented into countless tiny shards. I felt as though I was being turned inside out, as though my innards were extruding through my mouth. My body was apparently rolling on the ground (as I later realized), coiled into a ball like the ourobouros serpent. All distinctions between inner and outer, self and other, above and below, were obliterated. Animal sounds appeared to be coming from my mouth. There were no feelings of fear, indeed no feelings at all, other than a kind of impersonal ecstasy. No sense of body, no sense of self, no "I" – only a sparkling sense of awe-inspiring beauty (RM).

There was complete dissociative loss of awareness of my surroundings. However, apparently this disconnect was a function of my eyes being closed, because at one point I opened my eyes momentarily and could see that I was protected by my friends from bumping into things or rolling into the fireplace, in a kind of instant "reality check." Immediately after closing my eyes I was immersed again into the swirling, seething maelstrom of synaesthetic sensations.

Whereas Grof interpreted his experience in terms of the cosmology of Tibetan Buddhism, I attempted to make sense of my experience (afterwards) using the language of Vedanta, as well as Tantra yoga.

> There was a feeling of being in the nucleus of the psyche. Awareness of "all and everything" and simultaneously, "This is IT." The Vedantists say at the highest level

of consciousness there is only being (*sat*), consciousness (*chit*) and blissful joy (*ananda*). In my experience there was no self, no body, no time or space, but there was being. There was also consciousness: I could remember everything afterwards. Even though "I" wasn't there, there was observation and recording going on. And there was certainly bliss, joy, ecstasy unimaginable. I had the sense of being at an exact balancing edge between an internalizing and externalizing movement. I could let go, sinking deep within, falling and opening to a vast inner spaciousness, or I could let the energy come out and express through body movement and voice (RM).

I find myself on my knees, my body is being moved in incredibly smooth, fluid dancing motions, not by me, but by a spiritual Presence within me that feels totally other, unknown, not-me. Yet I don't feel any fear or resistance, just awe, as I willingly give over my form to be used by what seems to be a deity. I'm feeling my arms moving, and yet I'm not moving them. The presence feels now male, now female, now androgynous, now serpentine. *Shiva, Shakti, Kundalini.* The awareness emanating form this Shakti-being is all-embracing, all-encompassing of all of me, my body, and the environment. I remember experiencing what it felt like to be the floor that my body was resting on, the land that the house was on, the planet Earth that the land is on, the cosmos that the Earth is in…(RM).

Over the next several years, during the 1980s, I myself had a number of personal experiences, usually in small exploratory groups of two or three friends, smoking 5-Meo-DMT alone or in combination with DMT (in 1:5 quantitative ratio), usually with a vaporizer. We had dubbed the combined medicines the *Mayan Twins,* because the sudden onset of effects of the medicine, when inhaled, were reminiscent of the shape-shifting, shamanic trickster spirits in the stories of the Hero Twins, in the ancient Mexican

Popul Vuh. In these stories, the Hero Twins are able to defeat the terrifying Death Lords through allowing themselves to be repeatedly dismembered and killed and then shape-shifting back to their living human form.

From these early experiences, we realized very soon that it was extremely important, because of the dissolution of body boundaries, to have an agreed-upon ritual framework with clear space between voyager and non-ingesting sitter – or in a group, with clear boundary space between the participants. I remember in one early trial where I was lying near to a close friend as sitter, I found myself traveling through my friends digestive track, having inadvertently shifted my focus of awareness to the organ level, irrespective of body boundaries.

In another small group experience, my old friend RD and I had agreed to travel simultaneously, sharing the smoke from a vaporizer together, while a group of three others functioned as sitter-observers.

There's a swirling, weaving gridwork of light-patterns everywhere and all around. I can hear someone making choking and retching noises. RD was experiencing the vomit of the world's suffering, but was not suffering himself, as he later told us. At first I can't do anything – there is no "I" and nobody else. Then I notice that I'm being moved towards the sound, to reach out with my hand, to touch, to help, to give comfort. "I" didn't decide to do this, it just happened, sort of like an amoeba oozing over toward the source of apparent distress signals. My voice appeared to be making soothing sounds while my hands appeared to be making touching, stroking gestures. Awareness then arose of the other individual, this particular man, RD. Only after that awareness, came the realization that "I" was doing this gesture, this movement (RM).

It seemed (and seems to me still) significant that *the Other was recognized before the Self.* The human contact started with a response to the felt need of another being. First there was "Thou", then "Thou-I" relation, then "I." Object formation came before object relation. This experience confirms, I believe, the sequence of learning in infant development: the infant recognizes the other before the self, learns to say "Mama" before learning to say its own name or say "I."

Experimenting with the *Mayan Twins* combination in individual and small group experiences during the 1980s my colleagues and I gradually came to the realization that there was no particular advantage to including DMT in the vaporizer blend together with the 5-Meo-DMT. It only made for a more intense sudden onset, with vivid three-dimensional, moving kaleidoscopic patterns encompassing the whole visual field or even engulfing one's whole being. These kaleidoscopic patterns did not appear to have any particular meaning – it was merely a kind of abstract glitter, accompanied sometimes by images of strange, uncaring non-human entities, what Timothy Leary, in *The Psychedelic Experience*, had called "the retinal circus," or what Terence McKenna in his writings has called "self-transforming machine elves."

If images and thought-forms related to a person's actual human existence appeared, they tended to appear later in the session – and then only when the individual had some particular exploratory or healing intention. I remember once or twice having the distinct impression/sensation, after inhaling the combination, that I was waiting for the "retinal circus" to subside, as if it was some kind of film screen in front of my eyes, and when it did subside, there opened up a deeper dimensional field with meaningful scenes of people and spirits and landscapes. For these reasons related to the

content of the experience, and the practical reason of ease of ingestion, the experiences described below were predominantly with
5-Meo-DMT, inhaled through a vaporizer.

The context and set was always meditative and focussed
ultimately on spiritual understanding and healing. Many of my
experiences seemed to include cosmological visions and reincar-
national memories as well as personal healing processes, with the
cosmic predominating early, at the highest-deepest part, and the
incarnational-personal later, as the intensity subsided.

> Multi-colored lines of light formed a kind of dome
> covered in a faceted geometric network of jewels, the
> whole dome spinning silently. The jewelled dome seemed
> to become a kind of lens, through which I could see into
> other worlds beyond, where the points of light were stars
> and galaxies. At first there were tiny scintillating sparks of
> light against a velvety blackness. They merge to become a
> brilliantly colored, weaving, flowing tapestry of geomet-
> ric forms, extending infinitely in all directions. Then this
> kaleidoscopic field of patterns dissolved my body into it,
> so that I don't see it anymore – I have become part of it
> (RM).

A common theme in my experiences was an awareness of first
seeing a scintillating tapestry or lattice of multi-colored gems and
jewels and then merging into it and becoming one with it as it rolls
over me and through me so there was no more separate awareness
of body, of self, of things or of feelings. Although there is no sense
of self, at some point a kind of witnessing focus seems to appear.

I came to call the lattice-like tapestry, the "matrix of all possibilities." Reflecting on such experiences in the normal waking state,
I speculated that perhaps this lattice-matrix was a perception of the
molecular level of reality – where all is combinations and permuta-
tions of patterns and interconnections – no things, no objects, no
boundaries between inside and outside.

The weaving, waving field of geometric shapes and lines folds and falls over me, or I fall into it. I am seeing small spherical globules of white light, like pearls, that are glistening, shining moist, and perfectly aligned and interconnected in complex three-dimensional webs, reminiscent of Buckminster Fuller's dymaxion structures, yet always changing, unfolding and enfolding. These webs are what constitutes my body, clustering in certain areas to make organs like my eyes.

They also constitute all other bodies and forms around me. Each individual is a kind of cluster in this infinite ever-changing molecular web. Each thought or feeling or experience is also a local cluster in this holographic matrix of all possibilities. A sun of pure white light radiates out from the center of the swirling, pearl-studded crystalline grid. It is too intensely bright for me to maintain the focus of attention, so gradually I lose awareness of it and emerge back out of the infinite oneness back into my body-form (RM).

For some, this geometric lattice pattern may dissolve into primordial pure light or a formless void. Or, following the inhalation of the medicine, the experience may transition, synchronously with the exhalation, into a kind of blissful stillness. Cosmic patterns of stars and planets may permeate or oscillate with formless void visions. Here are some examples from accounts written by participants in our explorations with this medicine.

(Male) As my breath went out, I went in. And still I fell. The last vestige of resistance, a mere quiver of anxiety, subsided. I was fearlessly falling into an incredibly spacious, powerfully radiant, ancient but ever-present center, at once still and moving, a Core from which all things were arising, would arise, had arisen. I had let go and I had arrived. I was Home. That which I called "I" hung suspended in a vast, spacious and imperturbable Universe. I felt freed from my usual burden of aches, pains, tensions and fears, unconstricted, deeply and profoundly relaxed, at home in life, in a state of no struggle, deliciously, effortlessly healed.

(Male) I was somehow able to guide my body to a laying position, though I had very little body awareness. A deeper letting go seemed to occur by allowing the body to rest without muscular effort. All body awareness dissolved into awareness of soft, expansive currents of bliss. Even the sense of joy and amazement which this engendered dissolved as identity merged into formless Being. At that edge between Form and Formlessness, I felt the sense of being at a threshold which I had never before crossed. With both the joy and the difficulty of a birth, separate identity was relinquished, and all that remained was boundlessness. The relief and the sense that finally the ancient, primordial Search was over was utterly indescribable. There seemed to be an oscillation between pure undifferentiated Being and Observing Ego, because I had awareness of coming into Form, feeling profound ecstasy, joy, gratitude and love, and then dissolving back into That which from these feelings flowed. I became aware of a sense of arriving, of finally having found what felt like I had been looking for – for eons. I realized that where and who I am is self-evidently beyond life and death. A thought arose of my dying sister-in-law, and relief spread throughout at realizing the fallacy of death. A vague sound was associated with this relief, a wetness reminded me of bodily existence and I realized I was crying.

(Female) I experienced what I can only describe as pure awareness, though not self-identified. An awareness that travels in search of more, ever increasing, ever expanding and unattached – free of any limit, binding or density. It was pure awareness moving through space, though not like a dark starry sky, rather like the intervals between everything all combined. The "I" or "me" was gone. It was an experience of no individuality yet I had very definite awareness and full existence. I said

"I need help" – expressing a desire for the attention of others to enable me to focus, maneuver and navigate in such an unknown dimension. With the group attention, we journeyed to the "left-overs" of God, as Carlos Castaneda put it, or the outer limits of God. Then jointly we journeyed beyond, co-creating, co-realizing and traveling – exploring out into the very "nothing" beyond the universe, and then into the somethingness of form, like the energy of somethingness at the atomic or molecular level. We began recapitulating the evolution into form, rapidly entering all phases and kingdoms – the elemental, mineral, vegetable, animal...each with a new found awareness, understanding and capability. An experience of "Hey, look what I can do" of grand proportions. Each evolution finding itself, experiencing the opportunity of intention – particularly in the human form, and delighting in it, deliriously and hysterically. It literally cracked me up, through all the episodes of evolution.

(Male) At this point I was in an utterly empty place, where the only remaining thing was light itself. There were no features, not even a sense of energy flux. The place seemed as full as it could be, without containing a single object or pattern. Getting somewhere else, or waiting for a manifestation, simply did not occur to me. The guide later called this space the "plenum void", a term from mysticism that means the empty space that contains everything, a kind of featureless fullness. The basic nature of the experience was an initiation into the radiant void.

(Male) This medicine hurled me deep into the fiery firmament, with instantaneous, absolute death of ego, no-self on the quantum level of consciousness-chaos, harmony and bliss. The deepest fullest release from the chains of illusion. This big bang of God-orgasm, creation overwhelming bliss, no choice but absolute surrender to the primal current. Flooding back to consciousness, still fully aware as the body was permeated and open to the infusion of the ultimate ground of being. Body fully open to assimilate throughout every atom of being bliss-ful non-attached truth of the unlimited eternally fresh, fiery present. Left with a sense of unbounded joy and sensory delight beyond description.

(Male) Flying into a radiant ball of fire, the sun – entering it and plunging through it, coming out the other side, bouncing off the moon, landing on all fours on the moon, surrounded by giant space beings watching silently.

(Female) Unfolding of spatial structures and geomet-ric patterns. Then there is a bird, a swan, light and large, who flies with me over the Earth, and the Earth is so beautiful. The Earth looks as though set with pearls, daz-zlingly beautiful, and I have the thought "Oh my God, how beautiful it is." I am overwhelmed by the beauty of the Earth.

The cosmological visions one may have with this substance depend to a large extent on the pre-existing worldview of the person having the experience. James Oroc, in *The Tryptamine Palace* (2009) devoted a whole book to relating his profound life-changing mystical experiences with the smoking of 5-Meo-DMT, in which he was transformed from "a hardened atheist who embraced an inherited cynical material-reductionist worldview" to someone who is "indelibly aware of the existence of G/d." He writes that this first experience "was responsible for radically changing me into a spiritually inspired and much more hopeful human being" (Oroc, J. *op. cit.* p. 3).

The experiences Oroc relates include all the elements of the classic mystical, cosmic consciousness experience others have also related with the smoking of this substance: radiant white light, recognition of unity and love as the organizing power of Universe, complete dissolution of ego-identity, oneness with G/d, and a sometimes abrupt return to normal consciousness of one's body. After a year of self-experimentation, during which he smoked the substance two or three times a week, he unexpectedly had an experience of vivid contact and communication with a loved one who had died several years earlier. This experience expanded his worldview even further into previously unknown considerations of the after-life – and he "decided to take a break from tryptamine smoking for a while…to reflect on the possibilities that this experience had opened up." He stopped thinking of 5-Meo-DMT as a "drug," instead considering it a "sacrament of some kind" (Oroc, J. *op. cit.* p. 49).

Stanislav Grof, in his account, related receiving a whole series of death-and-rebirth visions of his past incarnations and witnessing the struggles of these past dyings with calm, even ecstatic detachment. Like Grof, I also found myself rapidly reviewing a series of past lives especially the deaths of these lives:

> Images of decapitation, dismemberment, disembowelment flashed by, in rapid succession, including an image of being run through the chest with a sword – yet there was no fear or horror associated with these images. The following thoughts occurred: "Death comes to all, now it's your turn. This is it, the termination. Resistance is impossible and pointless besides. It's too late, the annihilation has already happened." As I gradually came back into my body, after ten minutes in real time, I felt bathed in pure joy and completely at peace with myself, the world and my death (RM).

Speculative discussion

I have come to think, as stated above, that the 3-dimensional geometrical web, extending in all directions, that you first "see" in front of your eyes and then perceive as all-pervasive, inside and out, is the *molecular level of our physical reality*. Molecules of hydrogen, carbon, nitrogen, oxygen and various elements and compounds do not "know" or care whether they are inside or outside of your body, or associated with any object or form in the external world. There are no objects or bodies or boundaries at this level – there is only the totally impersonal, ever-changing network or web, crystalline lattices of replicating patterns. An image that comes to mind from Mahayana Buddhism is of *the jewelled net of Indra* – symbolizing a universe of infinitely replicating mutual interrelations among all things and beings.

Other researchers have come to similar conclusions, pointing to perception of microcosmic, molecular (and sub-molecular) realities as the interpretive key to the understanding of high-dose tryptamine experiences. In his recently published autobiography *The Brotherhood of the Screaming Abyss*, Dennis McKenna (2012), the ethnopharmacologist brother of the adventurous explorer Terence McKenna, eloquently describes a DMT-smoking experience he had, after a 15 year-hiatus in his psychedelic experimentations. In this experience there were none of the "self-transforming elfin entities" that his brother Terence had famously described. Instead the experience seemed to be a glimpse into the impersonal, no-thing-like, fragmentary "frenzied neurochemistry" of our own brains.

> All the elements were there: the frozen feeling bubbling up and permeating my body like quantum foam fizzing up to engulf the fragmenting mind, the feeling of acceleration, my

dissolving self urging me to let go, to surrender, as I was sucked into the visionary maelstrom. … The experience was far more austere (than in the earlier trials – ed.) Reality is a hallucination generated by the brain to help make sense of our being; it is made of fragments of memory, associations, ideas, people you remember, dreams you've had, things you've read and seen, all of which is somehow blended and extruded into something resembling a coherent conscious narrative, the hallucination we call "experience." Dimethyl-tryptamine rips back the curtain to show the raw data before it has been processed and massaged. There is no comforting fiction of coherent consciousness; one confronts the mind-less hammering of frenzied neurochemistry (McKenna, D., *op. cit.* p. 160).

Anthropologist Jeremy Narby, in his ground-breaking investigation of Amazonian shamanic knowledge systems involving the ayahuasca brew, similarly describes his working hypothesis as follows: "In their visions, shamans take their consciousness down to the molecular level and gain access to information related to DNA, which they call 'animate essences' or 'spirits.' This is where they see double helices, twisted ladders, and chromosomal shapes"(Narby, J., *The Cosmic Serpent*, p. 117).

Repeated observations by myself and others, have revealed that one can actually distinguish *two sorts of web-patterns*: one that is crystalline-geometric, with straight lines between nodes; another that is more organic and fibrous, with multiple branchings, like you might see in microscope images of slices of nerve tissue. The Pueblo Indian mythic image of *Spider Grandmother's* web of creation also comes naturally to mind.

Using the metaphor language of neurophysiology, perhaps in such experiences we're subjectively experiencing the *interface of neuronal nets and molecular grids*, "seeing" or "being in" now one, now the other. Nerve impulses travel along axons as sodium and potassium ions are pumped in and out of the nerve-cell membrane. Transmission across the synaptic cleft is by release of neurotransmitter molecules. There are 10 billion nerve cells in the brain; 100 million photo-sensitive rods and cones in the retina. So when you're "seeing" the grid-web, sparkling with jeweled luminescence, you're registering the activation of millions of the light-sensors in your retina. When you're sensing yourself embedded in the web, without distinction of "self" or "other," you're sensing being part of the cellular-molecular web of all life, extending infinitely in all directions.

In some of the experiences recounted above, there seemed to be an awareness, a subjective perception of even deeper levels of the microcosm – of atomic and sub-atomic quantum level and the ultimate void – expressed in phrases such as "primordial void," "ever-present center," "formless Being," "primary clear light," "ground of being" or "vast spaciousness." In the course of one 30 minute experience, the voyager's visions may oscillate between microcosmic web patterns and macrocosmic star formations, with personal (though not ego-centered) awareness – seemingly embodying the ancient Hermetic maxim – *as above so below,* and *as without so within.*

Spiritual shamanic healing experiences in group rituals

In general, we found that the most useful and valuable healing experiences tended to come later in the journey, as the initial intensity diminished, and one returned slowly and gradually into the customary body-consciousness, but carrying extended perception and blissful compassion into the physical form. Grof relates such healings in his published account. Here are some from my own initial experiences:

Something like a mask or blind over the right side of my face appears to be coming loose. I can feel the cheek muscles rippling under the skin, and facial nerves twitching, a sense of energy currents inside my body being aligned and balanced.

When I let go within, feelings of great peacefulness, a soft breathing in the heart, gently approaching knots of contraction or pain. Out of a hard nugget of pain somewhere, a serenely exploding flare of light energy spreads throughout the body. The softly ascending light flare consists of sparkling jewels and precious stones, as if the pain had been a locked-up treasure chest that was suddenly unlocked.

I am shown that if I can make certain sounds, the vibrations can actually disintegrate crystallized nuggets of pain or tension. Continued perception of ascending and descending glissandos, as if on a harp, but soundless, kinaesthetic, synaesthetic, soothing, healing (RM).

I began to participate in small group healing ceremonies with what we called the *Jaguar* process. We adopted this as a code name because the rapid onset of the medicine powder when smoked or inhaled was reminiscent of ancient Mayan mythic images of the open mouth of a jaguar, with the face of a human shaman looking out from within its jaws. Here are some accounts from these sessions which occurred in the 1990s and later, in the US and Europe, typically with 10-15 mg of 5-Meo-DMT, which would usually be inhaled in one draw from a vaporizer. As mentioned above, although we initially experimented with the combination of DMT and 5-Meo-DMT (the *Mayan Twins*), we gradually moved to using the latter alone.

The ritual form that developed was for two people at a time to be the self-chosen *voyagers*, sitting for the ingestion by vaporizer and then lying down in the middle of a circle of witnessing *guardians*, who would be silently meditating, creating a protective force-field. At first we also experimented with the guardians laying healing hands on the voyager – on the arms, shoulders, chest or legs. After a while we realized that the guardians tended to lay on hands based on *their* perception of what was needed. It was better to let the voyagers themselves experience the ecstatic free fall into the void of inner space – and reach out for a comforting hand only as desired or needed. To enable the voyagers to connect their experience with real-time, we would ring a bell and/or say that 5, 10 or 15 minutes had passed. People were typically astounded at how short the clock-time period was in which eons had been revealed subjectively.

After 15-20 minutes, a gentle pulling on the hands and feet could facilitate a smoother re-entry to full body awareness. Only at that time, after sitting up, removing blind-folds and looking at their friends, the voyager would relate their experience and the guardians also could verbalize their external observations. (This practice of sitting up, removing blind-folds and gazing into each other's faces, originated in the dissociative group experiences described below, pp. 54-55). Many voyagers spontaneously would make vocal (not verbal) sounds during the journey and find their limbs or whole bodies moving in gentle, flowing, yoga or tai chi like movements. This observation then also led to the practice of doing some yoga *asanas* both before the *Jaguar* session and again afterwards, during the re-entry phase.

The following account includes a formless void experience and terrifying dissolution, followed by profoundly healing integration, in which the voyager reached out to and was supported by a group of women friends – all within a 20 minute journey.

(Female) Within seconds of inhaling, the room filled with an amber-gold veil which seemed to coat everything. My entire body and mind were filled with visual, vibrational sound, which appeared like millions of tiny, flashing points of light. An intense swirling feeling came over my body and mind, and I felt a rapid and complete loss of control as I swirled downward into a very deep, bottomless whirlpool. I experienced a very sensual, unitive state with my partner (also voyaging). I experienced our essences blending like the mixing of water colors while still feeling each of us as individuals – he later confirmed something similar at the same point. As I swirled and lost control, a deep pain within me expressed itself as a high-pitched moaning that came screeching out of the very depths of me. I witnessed and felt this happening without capacity, or desire, to stop it from happening. With this sound I twisted and twirled downward, not knowing if my body was actually doing this or if it was a very strong inward sensation.

The next thing I knew, I was in a vast, dark space like a night sky, yet there was a slight whirling around me. I was no longer whirling, but the space around me was. My mind was fragmented into a million pieces which seemed to be floating around me in this space. I didn't know where I was or who I was. When I noticed this I felt lost and afraid. While there were no sign posts indicating a direction, I spontaneously made a kind of mental intention to go towards something and as a result began to move in a direction in this inner space. I then heard a deep, loving, feminine voice slowly say "That's right. You can do it." It was a voice from within this space, the voice of the guide. Upon hearing it, I was deeply, utterly relieved – her voice so soothing and warm, reassuring and firm. She felt ancient and familiar to me. I felt I knew what to do now, yet was overwhelmed with the task – I felt I was in an insane state of mind. While it felt like the most difficult thing I've ever had to do, I knew I had to move within this space in a certain direction.

There were no visual clues, only an internal sense that once I had moved that I was going in the right direction. I was going Home.

I heard a noise in the room and recalled where I was, that I was travelling with the *Jaguar*. I brought conscious attention to my breathing and gradually re-collected myself. I sat up and as I looked around the room at everyone I felt like Dorothy in the Wizard of Oz when she awoke from her long dream – I recognized everyone as ancient friends. I asked the women to form a cocoon around me and when they did I burst into tears and sobbed very deeply, accompanied by a very deep feeling of relief and return. I felt ancient connection and experienced a grounding and inner contact with my spiritual nature.

During the days following my journey, I alternated between anxiety and elation and experienced an amazingly broad range of levels of consciousness throughout my daily activities. I could easily perceive multiple levels of existence and experienced an increase in empathic and psychic ability. I also experienced a tremendous amount of sexual energy and greatly heightened orgasmic responses in my entire body. At quiet moments I felt very deeply relaxed and centered.

In the following account a man, who had through previous shamanic journey work developed a relationship with Jaguar as his power animal, reports feeling empowered to move into creating his own livelihood.

(Male) After moving into the space of formlessness, I felt directed toward my solar plexus area. It was very different than other experiences with healing body work – I was totally disidentified with my body, but somehow in it with a warmth of intention and orientation. I took a breath and a rippling of freedom passed through layers of mind out through the physical form. The pleasure of the experience brings waves of joy and a smiling feeling.

Jaguar emerged when I asked to open to his fierceness within me, to have the courage to move through fear blocks. Jaguar, my power animal, appears as I focus on a tightness in my upper back. He is biting me there, where I am contracting with fear and holding back. His energy is filling me, I am becoming him, moving my face and arms as a jaguar. It feels very good, very strong, uninhibited. Then I feel the courage to let go of my job (which I had been too afraid to do) and move into creating my own livelihood.

In the following account a woman relates how she came to a different and healthier relationship to the seizures she had been having.

(Female) I let go more fully than I ever have. I became the sounds and the movements – no controlling. That is the place where deep transformative healing takes place for me. It's also the place where Spirits meet to help others to heal. I felt like my voice and movement were healing and clearing the fear that I didn't need to hold anymore. It is the place where my seizures come from. The seizures are not an illness. They are an opening to other realms. My toning was multi-level. There was a woman's voice with an overtone of my child's voice and an undertone of my crone's voice. I could feel the tones working in my body, opening and releasing. There was only pure sound...no holding back. I found my full voice...I was being born, reliving my physical birth... releasing fear and opening to a new way of being in the moment. Allowing myself to enter the flow of life and humanity and move with it, not against it.

Such experiences reinforced in our minds the value and importance of having clear intentions and questions, whether related to healing or to cosmological exploration – rather than just taking a dose or a drug "to see what it does." It also confirmed, to my mind, that the 5-Meo-DMT medicine was preferable to the DMT by itself or in combination – because the slower onset and longer time duration allowed for a more meaningful process of seeking and receiving answers to one's personal questions or concerns.

Selective practice of body touch from others can be immensely healing. In groups it is extremely important, because of the extreme suggestibility of the state of consciousness, that possible touching during the experience is discussed and agreed upon beforehand, and that some kind of non-verbal code is worked out: for example, the voyager may reach out with their hand and this is the signal for the sitter or guardian to hold the hand, or place it on shoulder or chest, as guided by the voyager. After a certain time then, the sitter/ guardian should withdraw their hand, and let the voyager return to the complete inhabiting of their own space.

Because of the enormous expansion of one's sense of physical identity to include the subtle energy-field, it can occur very easily that you suddenly feel like you are literally and energetically inside the other – and this can lead to confusion about whether you are perceiving what is in you or in the other person. This is one of the reasons why, in our groups we have discouraged intimate couples from lying next to each other during the journey – because their energy-fields tend normally to be enmeshed with each other, and it is particularly illuminating and therapeutic to first experience your own inner space and subsequently conjoin them again. This is the dual paired process the old alchemists referred to as the *coniunctio* alternating with the *separatio*.

The intentional humming or vocalizing of selected mantras, as described below (pp. 56), either quietly to oneself, or audibly with the sitter/guardian, or by the whole group together, can have a wonderful effect of both expanding awareness and connection with others and with Spirit, as well as awareness of other beings and our connection with them.

Negative reactions and precautionary practices

In a comprehensive review of the pharmacology of hallucinogens David Nichols (2004) stated –

> Hallucinogens are powerful in producing altered states of consciousness, but they do so at doses that are not toxic to mammalian organ systems. There is no evidence that any of the hallucinogens, even the very powerful semisynthetic LSD, causes damage to any human body organ...Hallucinogens do not cause life-threatening changes in cardiovascular, renal or hepatic function (Nichols, D. *op. cit.* p. 134).

As Nichols and other reviewers of the medical research literature have concluded, though hallucinogens are not directly lethal by overdose, there is a potential danger of fatality by accidents due to impaired judgement or suicide due to dissociation accompanied by grandiose beliefs, such as that one can fly, etc. The most significant danger of all psychedelic drug ingestion stems from the possibility of triggering a psychotic or depressive episode in predisposed and unprepared individuals. Nichols concludes, "these drugs do not appear to produce illness *de novo* in otherwise emotionally healthy persons, but problems may be precipitated in predisposed individuals" (*op. cit.* p. 135).

My own experience confirms these general conclusions. Over a thirty year period, I have personally observed hundreds of sessions (many of them repeated with the same individuals) with these short-acting psychoactive tryptamines; and also read or heard from other therapists working in the informal underground network. I would estimate that dissociative, psychotic or fear-panic reactions have occurred in about 10% of cases. They tended to last at most a few minutes and dissipate as the intensity of the drug effect diminished, and the subject was able to recognize the reality of their surroundings, remember their intentional participation in the experiment and feel the support of the accompanying guides and friends.

Nevertheless, the disorienting dissociative experiences, when they do occur, can temporarily produce profound terror and discomfort – which has no doubt contributed to the somewhat fear-shrouded reputation of this drug. In an unpublished review I wrote up in 1990, about my then ten years of personal experiences with DMT and 5-Meo-DMT (separately and in combination), I estimated that about 10% of sessions had some negative or hellish component. Here is the portion of this report describing how such "bad trips" may typically develop.

> I get caught in a hell-world of some sort. In the initial phase, I'm aware of and merging with a kind of network of light, with a sense that this network or fabric contains all possibilities of experience. Each point of light represents a human experience, like what the Buddhists call a "seed-thought". One of these points could be "fear of dying." Things change so quickly, that this fear-seed usually doesn't develop into a full-blown panic state. But if I get fixated on it, or resist letting it pass, I get stuck and the movement stops. The shimmering network freezes and congeals: it becomes brittle, harsh and glaring, like steel wires and bands. It closes in on me, like an immense spider's web, tighter and tighter, as in Stan Grof's description of BPM-II. There is dread and terror associated with it and it can develop into a full-blown hallucination of a hell-realm. (These can occur with psilocybe mushrooms and LSD, too). It's a fully developed hell, with demons torturing me, reminiscent of concentration camp accounts or the torture chambers of the Inquisition. It has a historical feel to it, as if I'm a participant-observer of collective human history, since I know these are not personal memories from my life. Being aware of the possibility of such hellish experiences and centering preparation would definitely reduce the chances of getting stuck in them (RM).

The extreme potency of 5-Meo-DMT and the very narrow margin between an effective and a dissociative dosage made some of the early experiments, even among experienced explorers, subject to unexpected hazards. Careless estimating of dosages, even in a protective setting, can have serious consequences, as in the following account by a psychiatrist with considerable experience with various hallucinogens – in which dissociative phenomena continued, or re-appeared, after the apparent end of the actual trip.

No one knows the dose. We prepare the space around us for lying down. It is to be a roller coaster ride with no handles. Surrendering control, eschewing thoughts of control, going wherever the ride will take us—these are the guidelines. The friend (maybe not) with the stash says to me, "You are a big guy, have a big dose". He holds the silver spoon to my nostril and I inhale. A few seconds pass and so do I--into another realm. When I begin to come to, I discover my trip partner has been sitting astride me, apparently to minimize my thrashing. I am initially blank—a dark hole where experience should have been. I search for memory of my journey—and thankfully, it floods back, much like dream recollection.

I am at risk of dying. My energy has faded and I must re-invigorate or pass (out). My partner is naked on top of me urging me to come back. She is fucking me for life, using her love and sexuality to help me return. I am strengthening through her emphatic ministrations. Suddenly I burst orgasmically into the cosmos, lying on my back, floating in the star filled space, ecstatic, music from the movie Dune *playing. I am in the infinitude, immune to harm, voyaging in the great celestial abode. Both are happening simultaneously. And then, I begin to reenter—towards this world.*

And back I am. No, no actual orgasm. The trip continues mildly with consciousness for another short period. Other psychonauts have also landed and their recollections are variable—for some not much at all; for others a profound experience. We change positions and I feel awake, alert, and competent to handle sitting for my partner. The night ends with no casualties.

In this case, it was the delayed dissociative after-effects that were most troubling. On the day following the trip –

I am driving north to San Francisco, cruising along solo on vista-filled 280 when I suddenly notice that my head and upper torso are lying sideways on the passenger seat. Instantly alarmed, I pick myself up and pull over to the side. I have no recollection of my upper body having gone there. It must have been instantaneous, as I did not lose control of the car. It was a lapse of consciousness with automatisms continuing, in this case driving. I had control of the car with my hands, but my head was on the seat next to me with my upper body leaning over. It could only have lasted an instant or I would have lost control of the car and crashed. I remember righting myself, but not the going over that preceded it. I never recovered any knowledge of how I came to be on my side.

I am very anxious. My hands and feet are tingling. I wonder if something terrible is the matter with me. This is before the cell phone era. I drive slowly to a nearby rest stop, thinking that there will be a pay phone and I can call home. None. I don't want to use the emergency phone. No cops please. I am near the hospital where I am an attending psychiatrist. I could go there. But what would I say? That I had imbibed an unknown power-ful hallucinogen the day prior to my symptoms? Too awkward and risky. I could lose my privileges. I am a bit paranoid by now—very vulnerable. I leave, get back on the freeway and slowly drive home.

Six months more or less follow of a dissociative syn-drome. I have pins and needles in both upper and lower extremities, which with time diminish, fading first from the arms and hands, and finally the feet. The paresthesias are constant from awakening until sleep and I use a benzo to help induce sleep. There is also an oscillatory move-ment, like the shifting of a gestalt form, between being outside of myself and inside, my voice disconnected, as well as a tactile dissociation—it's not happening to a 'me.' At one point I am forced to discontinue providing therapy to a patient as it overwhelms me and I become extremely anxious and have to excuse myself for a sudden 'illness'. It worries me. I don't know when it will cease. Alcohol and marijuana make it worse, so I stop all use. I am unusually anxious. With time, I learn to accept the dissociation, to not be worried about it, that it is bearable and does no harm. And eventually it all fades and I am free of this aftermath. It was not until about twelve years later that I allowed myself to have another 5-Meo-DMT experience, this time at a measured low dose. I have had no other after-effects and consider 5-Meo-DMT to be an ally that teaches and provides new experience.

My colleague commented about his experience that it seemed "that the drug/mind interaction reassembled fragments of mov-ies I had seen previously and those movies were the substrate for the experience." For example, he mentioned the movie *Dune* in his account. One of my own experiences with the 5-Meo-DMT taken as a snuff resembled this kind of assimilation and "replay" of indirect experiences – in other words, experiences read or heard about that are incorporated and relived, as if occurring to oneself.

It was during the time when the story was in the news of the American Jewish girl who was run over in broad delight by an Israeli bulldozer demolishing Palestinian homes – an action she was protesting. I had read the story, sympathetically identified with the poor girl, but was not intentionally thinking about her at the time of this trial. Immediately after insufflation, I suddenly experienced myself lying on muddy ground and being crushed by an enormous bulldozer. There was no physical pain – just an unbearable feeling of sorrow and despair, while noting that my "body" was being crushed (RM).

This was one of many experiences that reinforced my practice of extensive concentrative meditation *before* ingestion. This is always beneficial, but essential with those medicines where the onset of the effect is very rapid after ingestion, within minutes or seconds. To start meditation after inhalation is obviously too late to find and establish one's psychic equilibrium.

Even if the dosages are estimated carefully and appropriately, the lack of prior experience with these substances, which involve unexpectedly rapid onset with strange and intense body sensations, can lead to difficulties if there are no experienced travelers present. I remember on one of my early trips in Europe, I introduced this substance (as a snuff) to a group of mostly women participants, about half of whom had a history of childhood sexual abuse as well as birth trauma, which they had worked on with various forms of intensive body and breath-oriented therapy. Only myself and the other guide had had prior experience with this particular medicine. In this group of women, many of the participants seemed to get stuck and were twisting their bodies into contorted postures and movements, along with much moaning and screaming. When I asked them to sit up as the drug effect wore off, they sat up, with their sitters by their side, and continued moaning and groaning for an unexpectedly long time after the drug effect would have worn off.

I was not worried for their safety, as I knew the drug was rapidly metabolized and the altered state would eventually wear off. I was wondering how it had happened that they seemed to calm down momentarily, at my urging, and then would start moaning, groaning and even at times screaming again, as they "stoked the fires" with heavy breathing. I realized that they were stuck in a repetitive groove in their inner process, and still had their eye-shades on.

I then asked them to take eye-shades off and look at their friend who had been functioning as sitter. The effect was dramatic – as the travelers recognized their friend and remembered that they had undertaken this experience for a healing purpose, they relaxed and smiled as tension and terror vanished. We then all sat in a circle huddled close together, holding each others arms or shoulders, looking at one another and quietly humming and chanting OM for another five or ten minutes.

This experience reinforced my conviction that it is a "best practice" to clearly mark the entry into and the exit from these dramatic shifts of consciousness – a practice well understood in cultures where the shamanic drumming journey is used, and also in those contemporary psychiatric settings where research with psychedelic substances is being conducted. An additional complicating factor in this group's experience was apparently the fact that none of the travelers had experienced this medicine before. I conducted a ceremony with the same medicine and similar set and setting shortly afterwards in another country, where about six of the ten participants had experienced the 5-Meo-DMT before. In this group there was none of the turmoil and fear, as new participants seemed to intuitively follow the unspoken lead of the experienced travelers.

I should add that my estimate of 10% fear-dominated "bad trips" is based on the groups I've observed, which consisted of seasoned adults, mostly with considerable experience with psychedelics, participating in small group settings with conscious intention and careful preparation. In more haphazard settings such as rave events or parties, with little or no preparation, the incidence of hellish bad trips is likely to be much higher.

In one of the early, more casual experiments I participated in with my friend Terence McKenna, using vaporizer-inhalation of pure DMT, I serendipitously came upon a method of getting out of such hell-realms.

As the shimmering fiber-nets became glittering steel-bands squeezing me (subjectively) to death, I found myself spontaneously making a kind of trilling sound – BRRRRR. I repeated it several times, each time more forcefully, and the sound produced a kind of "unzipping" of the steely armor that was constricting me. As it did, I shot from the depths of hell to the heights of liberated ecstasy. When I checked with my friend, he noted that the whole experience, from three inhalations of the smoke, the descent to hell and ascent to ecstatic heaven, took only about 3–4 minutes of "real time" (RM).

On reflection, I could see how my hell reaction was certainly in part a function of my lack of meditative preparation and somewhat casual approach at that time. In this particular exploration and other hellish or terror experiences that I've observed or heard described, in the literature or on the internet, there has been minimal attention to the factors of appropriate preparation, set and setting as well as the role of accompanying sitters or guides.

At the same time, I appreciated the unexpected teaching I was given concerning the salutory effect of this kind of sound-making – akin to the traditional Indo-Tibetan practice of mantra meditation. In fact, I've come to think that in the DMT hell experience, my inner spirit guidance was reminding me to use the seed-mantra RAM as a sonic centering device to help me find my way out of hell states. In general, we have found that the practice of mantra, especially single syllable seed-mantras like AUM or HUM or RAM, repeated silently or audibly, can be immensely helpful in terms of helping people stay centered and focused, when encountering fearful experiences.

In my book, *Worlds Within and Worlds Beyond* (2013), I relate how thinking or saying more complex mantras or prayers to oneself, in particular the ancient Biblical mantra I AM THAT I AM, can help someone find their way through and out of hell realms – as well as being a more general centering device for all kinds of experiences. A fairly conservative, though adventurous, psychiatrist to whom I introduced the 5-Meo-DMT snuff experience, prepared and protected himself from falling into fear by saying to himself a mantra-prayer he had learned from the *Course in Miracles* – "I am one with God and perfectly safe." A woman with extensive practice in Tibetan Buddhist meditation, centered and protected herself by visualizing and invoking the many-headed, many-armed deity image *Mahakala,* the embodiment of Time.

I believe that with these short-acting but profound consciousness-altering substances, with their inherent potential for inadvertent dissociative or panic reactions, it is a "best practice" to always have a familiar and experienced sitter or witness, who does not ingest the medicine. From my reading of the ethnographic literature on shamanic out-of-body practices with hallucinogenic plants or with the rhythmic drumming method, it is standard practice that the shaman who goes on a "flight" experience always has at least one assistant who watches protectively over his/her home-body while it is temporarily vacated, so to speak. In the shamanic worldview, if the body is unattended while the shaman goes on an out-of-body experience, there is a possibility of possession by a malicious entity or person. Although I have experienced these substances many times myself, I would never consider ingesting them without such a "ground control" companion.

Most of the groups I have known have made it a practice to do the inhalation ingestion in pairs: taking turns, with one person the voyager, and a second person acting as compassionate witness, providing reassurance and safety. In the majority of the exploratory groups in which I have been a participant-observer there has also always been at least one physician participant who is prepared to use life-saving procedures if these should become necessary; or at least one known to the group, living nearby, who has agreed to be "on call." Even when nothing untoward happens, knowing of their presence can serve to reassure the travelers and then this also allows for deeper insights and healings of difficult issues.

Possession states

Instances of apparent possession, whether by deceased other humans or non-human entities, are not considered "real" in the worldview of contemporary psychiatry and psychology – although they are recognized in the shamanic and folk-medicine traditions, and also in countries like Brazil, where there is a high degree of openness to considering both the beneficial and potentially malicious actions of "spirits." In *MindSpace and TimeStream* (2009), I wrote that obsessions, compulsions and possession states can be thought of as being on a continuum: in obsessions there is a repetitive series of thoughts, often self-critical and demanding, that the person can't seem to stop thinking; in compulsions there are in addition repetitive behavior routines, like repeatedly arranging and rearranging the furniture in a room or items on a desk. In possession states, the behavior and speech appears to be coming from some other person or entity – other than the host identity.

Full possession states, as in Haitian voodoo, fall at the extreme end of the dissociative spectrum, in that there is a more or less complete loss of ordinary awareness of the body and the environment;

and a sense of being taken over, voluntarily or not, by some other spirit or entity. There is usually no intention for the possessed individual to let him or herself be used for any purpose, such as healing, beyond the possession itself.

> From a psychological point of view, one could regard possession as a more extreme form of obsession, which itself can result from excessive attachment to a vision. A creative artist, inspired by a vision, may become obsessed with the challenge of bringing the vision into his/her chosen form of expression (*op. cit.* p.125).

> We are vulnerable to being controlled and taken over, to varying degrees, by feeling-states and thought-forms coming to us from others, particularly when we are in a dependency situation. Vulnerable dependencies may occur in childhood, during illness, or when there is an idealization projection toward the possessing person (*op. cit.* p. 127).

Possession states can be triggered in psychedelic drug states if the individual is predisposed to them because of their history, or because the set and setting of the experience is loose enough to trigger that kind of vulnerability. Some ten or more years ago, I witnessed an apparent instance of a temporary state of possession, during an experience with 5-Meo-DMT taken as a snuff powder. We were in Switzerland and the group of about 10 people were lying on mattresses in two rows on opposite sides of a fairly narrow room. Another psychotherapist and myself were guiding and not ingesting. The intention and verbal guidance given was meditative and towards psychospiritual healing. All the participants were moderately experienced with various other consciousness-expanding substances and had been working together for several days.

Shortly after insufflation of about 5-10 mg. of the snuff powder (dosage measurement was not yet very exact at that time), the woman in question, let's call her Barbara, started rolling from side to side and throwing her arms around herself, while moaning to herself with increasing loudness. Her eyes were covered by eye-shades, as were those of the other participants. As Barbara's movements became more and vigorous and her arms and legs were flailing wildly, the participants lying on both sides of her moved away for fear of being struck.

At about 30 to 40 minutes the experience of the other participants had subsided and there was clearly a need for some kind of intervention. Everyone gathered and sat around Barbara creating a space where her flailing arms and legs could not harm herself or anyone else. The group was asked to hum quietly and soothingly to Barbara, and channel purifying inner light-fire energy. I then asked her whether she was in her body, making these movements, or whether someone else was making them. She responded that it was someone else who was making her do this. I asked if she knew who it was and she said 'no.'

I asked her if she would consent if I talked to this possessing entity or being and she agreed. Taking my cue from Brazilian de-possession rituals I had seen, I asked four individuals who were relatively close to this woman to arrange themselves around her body – one holding her head, one on each side of her torso, and one holding her feet. The one holding her head and the one on her left-receptive side were instructed to channel purifying light-fire into her; the one seated on her right-dynamic side was instructed to magnetically draw toxic energy-elements out of her and consume them in their own field of purifying energy; the one holding her feet was also guided to draw the toxic energy-elements down and out of her body to be consumed. I didn't spend any time asking this entity to identify him or herself, but just insisted that he/she recognize that this was not his body, that he had no right to occupy it and that he should leave. This was said out loud, emphatically and repeatedly and accompanied by the purifying light-fire energy beams from myself and all the others.

We continued with this practice for some time and she gradually became quieter in her movements and utterances. She reported that the entity, whoever or whatever it was, seemed to have left her. She was shaken – as we all were. She related afterwards that a woman psychic whom she held in high regard as a teacher and healer, had advised her against working with mind-expanding drugs, due to her sensitive nature. She had decided to try them again anyway – but after this experience, stopped using such substances.

The following possession and de-possession experience was related to me by a physician/psychiatrist friend, who had been introduced to psychedelics as a college student studying epistemology and the philosophy of science, and stated that "one of my first experiences was so profound that it rendered all of my academic studies irrelevant." After a number of years in which he explored consciousness through psychedelics, meditation and yoga, he returned to school, obtained a medical degree, became a board-certified psychiatrist, and pursued a career in emergency and in-patient psychiatry with a public agency.

It was in this capacity that he encountered a young woman with a perplexing psychiatric history. She was hospitalized at the unit on which he worked due to sudden outbursts of extreme violence in which she severely injured other people or herself. Self-injury included fracturing her own bones. Between episodes, which appeared to be completely unprovoked, she was a sweet, petite young woman whose behavior, mannerisms, speech and thinking seemed entirely normal.

Diagnostically, she was an enigma, even after months on the psychiatric unit. She did not meet the criteria for psychotic illness or bipolar disorder and medical workups to evaluate for seizure or other neurological disorders revealed nothing which could explain her behavior. She continued to have sudden episodes of profoundly disturbing violence, and a number of the hospital staff were injured. Medications seemed to have almost no benefit, and at times required physical restraint. One day a nurse commented that if ever she had encountered a case of possession, this was it.

During this period, my psychiatrist friend was working with a "medicine circle" of several colleagues, who were using 5-Meo-DMT and other psychedelic substances in a healing and exploration context. This group of explorers, with which I sometimes participated, had a minimal structure of staying together in the room in the circle. But everyone took the medicine and no one was guiding or even sitting as "ground control." Participants were intermittently talking and interacting. I was myself not in agreement with this structure, which I considered below minimum – and for that reason actually left after some hours, finding the situation too chaotic to produce any useful outcome.

On this occasion, my friend who was treating the disturbed young woman, related that as the effects (of the 5-Meo-DMT snuff) became evident,

> I began to hear what I can only describe as 'malevolent intonations.' It clearly sounded like language, although none that I had ever heard, and the energy was chillingly malevolent. I felt as though I was under attack and I responded by psychologically 'hunkering down.' I don't have a clear memory of what followed. Other circle members tell me there was a period in which I thrashed about on the floor and was completely internally focused so that no communication with them was possible. I

have fragments of memories in which I felt as though I was in some kind of epic battle, and at times spirit energies seemed to come into my body. One of these was Jaguar, a personal totem, which I remember filling my body, being present for moments in the room, and then leaving. Eventually, I started to regain normal consciousness, but I felt tired and out of sorts.

The experience was certainly not what I had previously experienced with this medicine. The next day I went home, still feeling off. When I got home, I was puzzled by the behavior of my dog, with whom I was very close. Normally, he would greet me with enthusiastic affection, as though I had been gone for months, but on this day he seemed reserved and would not get near me. Over the course of the next few weeks, I came to recognize that I was out of sorts with virtually everyone in my life. There was uncharacteristic tension between my brother and I, with my wife, and at work. My coworkers, who were used to my usually calm demeanor, commented that I seemed bothered or upset. And strangely, my dog continued to avoid me. I began wondering what was going on, and had to ask myself—was I going crazy? It was just so weird, how suddenly everything had shifted and all of my relationships, even with my dog, had soured.

I continued to work on the psychiatric unit, including treating the young woman mentioned above, who continued to have paroxysms of violence. I was vaguely aware of feeling tense and irritable, and could tell that I responded to people and circumstances in an uncharacteristic manner, but I had no idea how to think about this. One day, about three weeks after the medicine circle, I was home alone, soaking in my hot tub. I was reflecting on the matters I'm describing, and candidly, I was really beginning to wonder if I was losing it.

Suddenly, I became aware of the same malevolent energy which had been intoning at the medicine circle. I don't recall actually hearing the intonations this time, but

I clearly recognized that the same energy that had been the source of those sounds was present with me this day, as I sat in the hot tub. Immediately, I knew what needed to be done. I very directly gave my attention to this presence and once it was fixed in my awareness, I said with great authority, "You're not welcome here. Leave!"

What I experienced next was an immediate sense of something lifting off of me. I felt light and suddenly unburdened. And I realized that I now felt alone in a way I had not been feeling the previous weeks. This evoked a dawning realization and an extraordinarily creepy feeling that I had been raped. I felt disgust and revulsion, and a deep sense of having been profoundly violated. I was at a loss about how to think about this. As a psychiatrist, this all seemed very crazy, but I had to acknowledge that the most intellectually honest response was to recognize that, whatever they meant, these were my experiences.

Over the next few days, my friend quickly saw that, with regard to relationships, things were back to normal. His wife and co-workers commented about this, and his dog was back to his usual unbridled affection. What was not back to normal was the behavior of the young woman he had been treating. All of the violent episodes stopped. In one week, after months on the unit, and with no change in her medications, she was able to be discharged. He was told by a co-worker who still worked with the department, that she has never been re-hospitalized.

The two experiences had in common the observation and diagnosis of possession – a condition not recognized as real in contemporary Western psychiatry and psychology. The improvised successful de-possession treatment in both instances lends credibility to the reality of the condition and the diagnosis. The fact that one possession state occurred during a trip in a very chaotic environment and later took three weeks to resolve, whereas the other was healed right away, confirms the importance of a peaceful and meditative ritual structure, with non-ingesting participant-observers, in which such unusual and potentially dangerous experiences can be identified and contained.

Abusive guide behavior

A different kind of danger with these substances, as with other psychedelics, is that the power and depth of the experience can potentially prove seductive to those who provide them. I know personally of two instances where reckless ingestion behavior on the part of the provider and supposed guide had very serious consequences.

In one situation, the provider, a chiropractor with a history of inappropriate sexual advances toward clients, inhaled 5-Meo-DMT together with two women, one of them his fiancée, by the side of a hot-tub in a private residence. They had also been experimenting with prolonged breath-holding under water. The fiancée submerged herself in the pool after ingestion and floated, while the chiropractor and the other woman, both also ingesting, lounged by the pool-side. After about five minutes in the deepest, ecstatic, time-less phase, the chiropractor suddenly realized the woman in the pool was floating face-down in the water. The others rapidly pulled her out and attempted resuscitation, but it was too late – she had inhaled water and drowned. Because of the rapid metabolism of these tryptamines, no drugs were found in her system, and the death declared accidental.

The other situation involved a psychiatrist who, also tempted by the brevity and depth of the healing trance, started ingesting the medicine by vaporizer inhalation himself, several times a day, before and during sessions with his clients, to whom he also offered it. On one occasion he had smoked the medicine just before opening the door to this waiting room – and grabbed the breasts of his next woman patient, supposedly perceiving her as "The Goddess." Although the drug itself at that time was not prohibited, these egregious professional boundary violations were eventually reported by several of his clients, and he was stripped of his medical license.

Of course, ethical lapses and professional missteps have also occurred with other psychoactive medicines, and indeed with all psychiatric medications and psychophysical treatment modalities, especially those involving bodywork. Nevertheless, I feel it is incumbent upon me to mention this cautionary note. Nothing in what I am writing here about what I have learned from explorations with these substances should be construed as my advocacy of their use by anyone. They are extremely powerful mind-altering substances, indeed entheogenic sacraments, and should be approached only with collaborative caution, experienced guidance and respect. At the same time, my unsystematic field observations from the underground culture certainly deserve to be followed up with more systematic research projects.

The snuffing method of ingesting 5-Meo-DMT

Almost all of the experiences described above, which occurred during the 1980s and 1990s, and the vast majority of the experiences in published and internet writings about DMT and 5-Meo-DMT involve inhalation of the medicine as a smoke (on a base of mint leaves or cannabis) or, more often, through a vaporizer. Through his writings and through conversations with Jonathan Ott, who describes himself as a "pharmacognocist," I myself and other explorers and researchers interested in this area became aware that it is possible to safely ingest the purified substance 5-Meo-DMT as well as other psychoactive tryptamines as snuff, and with considerable more ease than the Amazonian shamans who snuff the dried plant powders through long blow-tubes (Ott, J., 2001).

An effective dose of 5-10 mg of 5-Meo-DMT can be inhaled into the nasal passage with a straw, in one inhalation, with minimal and transient burning sensations. This amount is visually about the size of a few grains of salt – and cannot be accurately estimated with the naked eye. The small size of an effective portion of this medicine has the advantage of ease of ingestion, but the accompanying disadvantage that it is easy to ingest an overdose, producing dissociative panic reactions in naïve or unprepared individuals. As stated above (p. 24), the *ED-50* of 5-Meo-DMT is 5 mg and the *DD-50*, at which 50% of subjects dissociate, is 15 mg. Careful measurement of these minute doses is therefore highly advisable – one could even say essential.[2]

The major advantage of the snuffing method of ingestion is that the experience lasts 45 minutes to one hour (compared to 10-15 minutes with the vaporizer inhalation method) – leaving ample time for meditative, therapeutic or shamanic practice, supported by recorded music or chanting or drumming. My colleagues and I were affirmed in switching to this as the preferred mode of ingestion when we realized that snuffing is the method the Amazonian Indians use for this medicine, for whom the powdered plant material is forcefully blown into the nostrils.

A further advantage of the snuffing method of ingestion over smoking is that onset of action after insufflation is about 5-7 minutes. This is because adsorption of the powdered material through the mucous membranes of the nose takes slightly more time than

---

[2] Measuring spoons for amounts of 5-10 mg. of any crystalline powder can be obtained on the internet.

absorption of the inhaled vapor through the lungs. This leaves more time for meditative centering and lessens the likelihood of dissociation due to anxiety at the suddenness of onset.

In comparing ingestion by smoking/vaporizing with ingestion by snuff, the most significant difference between DMT and 5-Meo-DMT also becomes apparent. It is hard to come by much information of the effect of snorting crystallized pure DMT. Few people seem to have found this method of ingestion useful because to snuff an effective dose of 50-60 mg. would be a laborious and painful (to the nasal passages) procedure. If you could do it at all, the effect of the snuffed DMT would last about 30 minutes, though I suspect few people are willing to put themselves through such discomfort.

As mentioned above, we had adopted the protective code name *Jaguar* for this shamanic medicine, and on my own first trial with the snuff method, after several years and dozens of trials of only working with the smoking or inhalational method, telepathically received an affirmation from the spirit of Amazonian shamans, in the form of the statement – "Jaguars don't smoke." Like other cats, they avoid smoke and fire – but also like other felines, they do constantly sniff and snuff the surrounding chemical atmosphere.

My personal view is that the smoking/vaporizer method of ingesting this substance has no advantages whatsoever over the ingesting by snuff, and several drawbacks, as indicated above. Negative dissociative and panic reactions can and do still occur with the snuff method, but can be considerably reduced through meditative preparation, a supportive, non-ingesting guide or sitter, clarity of intention and very careful measurement of the minute doses involved.

A further refinement of the ingestion procedure that reduces negative reactions to virtually zero is to take an initial insufflation of about 5 mg, a threshold dose, and then, after 20 minutes or so, when the full effect of that amount is felt, an additional dose of 5 – 10 mg can be taken, by choice, for deeper healing work. This then produces a depth healing trance lasting about 90 minutes or so, with ordinary real-time awareness of one's body and the surrounding space returning gradually and peacefully.

While the deep, out-of-body states of cosmic consciousness described above with smoking doses of 15 mg and above can and do also occur at these dosage levels, they are less common. Nor do they seem to be necessary to produce deep healing and insight experiences – which typically occur as the person returns to ordinary time-space awareness.

Rather than a dissociated out-of-body trance state, as can occur involuntarily in trauma, and as can also be used intentionally in hypnotherapy, where the person doesn't remember anything on returning – these are *absorptive trance states* where awareness remains in the body but is simultaneously expanded into extra-dimensional and infra-somatic realms, and with full memory on returning. We have found also that having and holding the intention to remember the experience enhances the re-membering, thereby connecting the deeper realizations with everyday consciousness.

The following poem was inspired by my experiences with the *Jaguar* medicine of slowly descending to deeper levels of body consciousness in an intentional, conscious healing trance. I titled it *Diving for Treasures – Absorption*. It was recorded in my CD of spoken word poetry, *Spirit Soundings*, accompanied by beautifully evocative music by Kit Walker and other friends.

Here, in the cave of the heart, slowly,
the soul's eye descends to the depths,
crystal diving sphere,
omnidirectional lens,
scanning organic inner realms,
cellular mother ocean bed,
molecular web and net,
interconnected to infinity,
pulsing vibrational streams,
Light! Darkness! Light!

You are seeking the pearls
of golden energy-essence,
guarded by the dragon,
dwelling in the labyrinth of memory.
That dragon's name is
pain-fear-threat-scream.
Speak softly to that dragon,
Or sing to him soothingly, like Orpheus.
Then, you may take the precious pearls
from his frightful, flaming jaws.
You must thank that dragon,
for guarding them so well.

Or, you may find the sunken ship,
forgotten, with caskets of treasures,
gifts from the angels of childhood.
Or, you may find them buried,
under the sands of time and of sleep.

The diver gathers these precious jewels,
these stones of wisdom,
these sparkling elemental essences—
brings them to surface awareness,
into the light-filled cave of the heart.

From there to the soles of the feet,
for the understanding of that which is;
and to the crown of the head,
for the vision of what may be.

Use of the Jaguar snuff to amplify spiritual healing

In my view, the primary and most valuable applications of the *Jaguar* snuff medicine, as well as other entheogenic substances, are to amplify and support meditative practices with an implicit or explicit agenda of healing, i.e. furthering the wholeness and integration of the spiritual, mental, emotional and physical domains of our beingness. As mentioned above, I've observed that the more experienced someone one is in meditation practices, the more likely s/he is to be able to preserve a centered perspective, from which healing and insight-producing movements of consciousness can occur. I don't see any point or value in ingesting this substance (or any substance), just "to see what it does." The substance, after all, doesn't really "do" anything – rather, the biochemical changes produced in the brain permit the shamanic-alchemical practicioner to amplify their healing and visioning practices.

From my observations in the underground entheogenic subculture in the US and Europe, there are basically two kinds of ritualized ingestion practices: (1) one person is a guide, experienced both in meditative practice and with the amplifying medicine, who conducts a sacred ceremony, though not ingesting him/her self; (2) a small group of people come together by agreement, roughly equally experienced in meditation and the use of amplifying substances. Here it is also a best practice if one person does not ingest and remains as a kind of "ground control," being available to support the others as needed and monitoring the dosages taken, so that this factor does not become subject to hallucinatory distortion.

I have been in groups of peers, where everyone ingested at will, situations that tended to quickly degenerate into chaos and confusion, with increased likelihood of panic episodes and little useful outcome. On the other hand, I know of groups of colleagues and friends, equally experienced, who meet for sacred ceremony once a quarter or once a month or once a year, rotating the role of the "keeper of the sacrament," to minimize the possibility of inadvertent overdosing (which, as we have seen, is extremely easy in the case of this particular medicine).

A useful formula for planning amplified sacred ceremonies is to spend approximately equal amounts of time in preparation beforehand and integration afterwards, as for the medicine experience itself. Thus, for the *Jaguar* snuff experience lasting 45 minutes one would practice meditative attunement for 45 minutes before and have 45 minutes of integrative discussion and sharing afterwards.

Each person or group can and would of course practice meditation in their own accustomed way. Basic mindfulness practice, the continuous observing of breath and continuous observing the passage of thoughts and feelings, does wonders to calm the agitated and anxious mind. I have heard of Jewish groups in which prayers and invocations based on the Kabbalistic Sephiroth Tree were used to enhance the spiritual depth and direction of psychedelic experiences.

In my book *Alchemical Divination* (pp. 59-74), I described the light-fire yoga meditations that I practice and teach, in addition to the basic mindful continuous observing of the stream of consciousness. They involve:

(1) invoking purifying light-fire energy in the heart-center and expanding it from there throughout the body and field (the alchemical *purificatio*);

(2) intentionally balancing the receptive-left and dynamic-right sides of the body and inter-penetrating energy-field;

(3) channelling this light-fire energy-process throughout the upper centers of the head and throat to purify mental or thinking awareness;

(4) channelling the light-fire energy throughout the centers of the chest, heart, solar plexus and upper abdomen to purify feeling and emotional awareness; and

(5) channelling the light-fire energy throughout the lower abdomen and pelvic bowl, to purify sensory and instinctive body-awareness.

Preparation, integration and hatha yoga practices

The basic postural sequence in medicine circles with a spiritual orientation is to practice prior meditative attunement sitting in a circle, ingest the medicine powder by snuff with a straw, and then lie down for the duration of the journey, with eyes closed or covered, to focus on the interior visions. The music being played or guided meditation provided would all be worked out and agreed upon beforehand, or left to the guide, so that no "this world" decisions or choices need to be made by the voyager during the interior journey. At the end of the journey with the *Jaguar* in the two-stage ingestion process described above, after about 60-90 minutes, the participants sit up again and share experiences and learnings. For group cohesion and clarity of the ritual structure it is best if the time course of the journey and booster dosing is left to the guide, or as agreed beforehand, so that people can return from the inner journey at roughly the same time.

Over a period of time, working with individuals and in small groups with the snuffing method, which induces experiences lasting up to an hour, we learned that one of the most remarkable pharmacological effects of this particular medicine seemed to be an enormous increase in the ability to relax skeletal muscles. Slow movements of an arm, a shoulder, leg or hip are accompanied by hugely pleasurable sensations, as if the joints were lubricated with some kind of silken lotion. Yoga practicioners could assume stretching postures with ease and pleasure that normally would be accompanied by stressful tension. I speculated that somehow the drug seemed to have a specific facilitative action at the neuro-muscular junctions, where nerve fibers send neurotransmitter messages to skeletal muscles to relax. As mentioned above (page 21), this effect, if confirmed, could potentially lead to the development of new treatments for neuro-muscular diseases like myasthenia gravis. The immediate drug effect wears off, of course, but the some of the increased flexibility can linger for days, and stay somehow in somatic memory.

The groups in which I've been a participant-observer, started to include practice of some basic yoga postures (*asanas*) as preparation for the experience, such as the slow mindful turning of the head from side to side, the cat *asana* (appropriate for a jaguar!), child *asana* and downward-facing dog *asana*. We would practice the postures beforehand in the normal waking state and then repeat them once the medicine started to take effect. Of course we only did this with the postures in which you are sitting or lying on the ground – and not with the standing postures, which would be too challenging. With this comparison it was easy to observe the enormously heightened flexibility and pleasurably sensuous quality of movement when the drug effect had take hold.

From text-books on hatha yoga, I had learned that the child asana – in which you are on your knees on the ground, curled up with your head at your knees and your hands at your feet – is also called the "embryo asana." In this posture the body is closely packed together in the overall shape of a papaya or avocado. One time, when practicing yoga postures with the *Jaguar* medicine, I assumed the child or embryo posture, and suddenly felt my body-image shrink step-wise to the body-image of a child, an infant, a fetus, an embryo and then a single cell! As soon as I recognized this, the body-image moved step-wise back up the developmental ladder to my usual present adult self. The whole double process of regression and return had probably happened within 30 seconds or maybe less.

I was impressed, not only by the ability of this particular asana to trigger this kind regression to embryonic awareness, but by the ancient Yoga masters, who must surely have known this capability, and named the posture accordingly. From then on, we have made practicing hatha yoga along with meditation part of the preparation and initial stages of the *Jaguar* journeys. I can recommend this practice very highly. Once the medicine starts to fully enhance interior somatic awareness, it is best to remain lying down in what is called in yoga the "corpse asana" – suggestive of the complete release of awareness from identification with the physical body. As an alternative to hatha yoga asanas, the slow and gentle movements of tai chi could also be used by way of preparation for heightening body awareness – although not of course during the journey itself.

Amplification of pre- and peri-natal experiences

In my book *The Life Cycle of the Human Soul (2011)*, I described the trajectory of pre-natal and post-mortem human existence, drawing on experiential evidence from five main sources of empirical observation: psychedelic experiences, meditation and yoga, shamanic journey methods, non-ordinary breathing practices and hypnotic trance states. I draw extensively on the pioneering work of Stanislav Grof, who, through his initial work with LSD psychotherapy discovered and described key features of the birthing experience and how they affect child and adult character structure and psychopathology. Grof later developed an intensified breathing method, called *holotropic breathwork*, to access such deep unconscious and transpersonal realms without drugs.

In the 1990s I came into contact with the work of William Emerson and other body-centered healers and therapists who work with the imprinted residues in adult consciousness of prenatal experiences, all the way back to conception and even to pre-conception soul memories. I took a number of workshops with Emerson, who combines intensive breathing methods with pressure and weight on particular areas of the body to elicit early, pre-natal memories lodged deep in cellular tissues (Linn, S. F., *et. al.*, 1999).

I engaged in three ten-part series of body- and breath-work sessions with different practicioners, focussed specifically on releasing peri- and pre-natal armoring patterns, which I found very helpful. Some of these were conducted floating in a warm-water environment, with a snorkel for underwater breathing – which simulated even more closely the conditions of intra-uterine existence.

I did not myself use 5-Meo-DMT or any other substance during these sessions. But I did notice that my experiences with psychedelics, including particularly 5-Meo-DMT, made accessing the birth and prenatal body-memories by these other, non-drug methods that much easier. This confirmed for me the conclusion that these prenatal experiences were not "drug-effects" or "breathing effects," but that we were accessing an innate developmental memory system by different methods.

In *The Life Cycle of the Human Soul*, I relate the experience of a participant in one of the studies when we were using the *Jaguar* as a snuff. A woman reported re-experiencing simultaneously her own birth, herself giving birth to her child and sexual orgasm. The pelvic contraction-relaxation pulsations were somehow overlayed or interlayed with the sensation-memories of these three core experiences of her life. I noted that such fused experiential memories have also been reported to occur with non-drug methods such as holotropic breathwork (*op. cit.* p. 27).

I had occasion to participate in a series of deep prenatal healing sessions using the *Jaguar* snuff with a practitioner experienced and trained in the gentle body- and breath-oriented approach used by William Emerson and others. We assumed the different roles of *guardian* and *voyager* and exchanged them after an hour. This was analogous to the way a deep-sea diver might have someone at the surface, monitoring their safety and with supportive touch as requested.

The other therapist and I found these explorations profoundly healing, especially in regard to traumatic memory imprints of shame and pain lodged in deep recesses of the subconscious body-mind. Experiences such as these led me to the general conclusion that if deep healing is the primary purpose of the work, then working individually like this is probably the best way. Furthermore, working with pre- and perinatal trauma imprints should only be undertaken by those therapist-guides who have received training in this specialized field – which is not one included in the curricula of ordinary psychiatry or psychotherapy.

Healing experiences can of course also occur in group ceremonies – even although there the primary intention is deep meditative absorption – and it is usually not possible or advisable to specifically focus on releasing deep-seated traumatic memory imprints. In one of our group ceremonies with the 5-Meo-DMT snuff, a woman therapist with much prior experience with deep altered states and pre-natal regression therapy, related a partial resolution of a long-standing birth trauma.

> The *Jaguar* session was very hard for me. I went almost immediately to a place of absolute despair. I was overwhelmed with a surreal sense of aloneness that was so dark and deep that I was not sure of my existence. Then I looked around and realized I was in the birth canal. Next I did an internal scan and realized I had no impulse to be born. (Later I reminded myself that my mother was anaesthetized for a forceps delivery, so in hindsight that perception-memory makes sense). Tuning in to the post-partum phase, I felt no one was there. This started a series of flashbacks. The memories were of the most intense periods of despair throughout my life. The background of these intense moments was an entrenched theme of surreal apart-ness, that lacked even the self-awareness to feel lonely. I asked my She-Wolf ally for help as this state ruptured into tears. Next I am being held. To my surprise I recognize that I am not alone. An invisible separation wall came down, allowing me to be in contact with life. This was a totally new experience for me, to my delighted astonishment.

On one *Jaguar* group journey, a voyager previously experienced with holotropic breathwork and other modalities, found himself healing the residual trauma of a medical abortion he and his partner had reluctantly chosen. It was a powerful healing experience that deepened his compassionate commitment to his path as a therapist.

> During the journey we did with the *Jaguar* I went deeper into various aspects of my birth and early postnatal phase. Something very peculiar happened while I was re-experiencing the separation from my mother: what I

perceived to be myself suddenly merged with the soul and body of the fetus my partner and I had thought was to become our child. During the fifth month of pregnancy it turned out that the baby wouldn't be able to live because it had the liver outside the abdomen, a genetic malfunction that happens about once in a thousand pregnancies. We were advised to abort the child, but that entailed my partner being administered labor inducing medication which would lead to the death of the child. Now, it is easy to imagine what kind of guilt feelings this predicament potentially incurs. We did a lot of ritual around the decision, then both went to the hospital, stayed there for 48 hours, and had a hands-on experience, literally, of how the baby slowly stopped moving in her womb after the medication was given. When the 'birth' was completed, the doctors had left us alone and we both held our child, looked at it, spoke to it, loved it and then called the doctors back in, who took it away. It was a girl and would have become our daughter. We later learned that at exactly the same hour my grandmother, aged 96, died. In a vision received several days later I saw them leaving hand in hand.

The feelings during this process seemed to me and my partner about as much as a human being can endure, if not too much. Did we kill? This question, thanks to the ritual we did around the whole process, never really took over but it did at times trouble us deeply. So, during my *Jaguar* journey I mysteriously merged with this being, seeing and feeling its suffering, looking ahead at a life that wouldn't be livable. At some point in the process, my consciousness still at one with the being that would have become our child, but at the same time seeing the immortal soul of this being, I was able to ask – "Did we kill you?"– upon which the immediate reply came with the deepest compassion for our worries and a profound gratitude towards me and my partner: "No you released me, and for that I will be grateful to you forever, and when you encounter hardships and fears in your journeys I will always be there for you."

In sharing this profound healing experience with the group the next day, I accessed a depth in my grief for this daughter of mine and for my partner who had to endure all this, both on the soul level and inside her body, that I never had been able to get to before. The deeply compassionate and loving support I received from the group and the teacher made it possible for me to dare show what I feel. But the gratitude for being given this experience was overwhelming and even greater than the grief: I had found an ally, a powerful and committed guide for future healing work.

I should emphasize here that although birth and prenatal memories can and do arise spontaneously during psychedelic experiences, where they can be worked with by individuals and practitioners sensitized to them, I do not believe it is appropriate and perhaps even counter-productive to combine forceful breathing or bodywork methods with entheogenic substances such as 5-Meo-DMT (or ayahuasca, psilocybin or LSD for that matter). These intensive breathing and body-methods use dynamic energy to break through conditioned inertia-resistances imprinted into the cellular and organ tissues of the body. The subtle high-frequency energy perceptions possible with entheogenic amplified meditation may be overwhelmed and overshadowed by the lower-frequency but high-intensity body sensations and tension-release movements.

On the other hand, alternating the different methods of accessing deep unconscious body memories on different occasions, comparing findings and consolidating healing changes, can of course be very valuable. I know, for example, that some holotropic breathwork practitioners who are also familiar with entheogenic media such as ayahuasca, have practiced the two different methods on different days.

Of course, mindful breathing practices are always beneficial, in every state of consciousness. "Conscious breathing is the master key to healing," as the ancient saying goes.

Rebirthing and healing experiences in water

In my search for productive healing applications of the *Jaguar* medicine, I also had occasion to experiment with it in conjunction with water-flotation re-birthing methods. I held some group workshops at a center in Oregon, where there were large warm-water pools and practitioners experienced in the method of holding someone who is floating and breathing with a snorkel at and below the water level – a near-perfect evocative simulation of intra-uterine oceanic oneness.

We worked out a system where all the participants experienced being held in this way and learned to hold and support another person. Each person also first experienced the *Jaguar* snuff on dry land, with support. Then, by choice, those who wanted to could take the snuff (in a very mild dose) and then again be held floating in the warm water pool. At no time was there even the slightest hint of any fear or distress on the part of anyone – the experience for all was one of incomparably peaceful deep relaxation, in a unity of body, heart, mind and Spirit.

Having said that, it may surprise the reader that nevertheless I don't see any particular reason to pursue or repeat that kind of combined practice. The experience of water-flotation supported by a re-birthing healer is profound enough and so is the experience of working with the *Jaguar* medicine, with the appropriate spiritual healing set, support and preparation. My reticence to advocate for combining these modalities is supported by my awareness that obvious dangers do exist in these situations, if they are not approached with the utmost respect and caution. Alternating them on different occasions on the other hand could yield valuable complementary insights, as indicated above for the holotropic breathwork method.

Conclusions

I believe the descriptions and commentaries on this powerful visionary medicine make it clear that here is an area of research on healing that if pursued earnestly and carefully could yield results of enormous benefit and potential applications in the alleviation of physical, mental and psychosomatic illnesses and distress.

I believe I have also made it clear that it is essential that those practitioner/researchers exploring the applications of this approach themselves experience these modalities in their own person, without fear of ostracism from their community of colleagues and research institutions. It is a major blockage in advancing the understanding and application of the consciousness-expanding healing methodologies – that the officially approved research projects are required to adhere to an inappropriate protocol that prohibits or discourages such so-called "subjective contamination". In my book *MindSpace and TimeStream (2009)*, I argue that Western science and medicine needs to break out of its self-imposed methodological strait-jacket and adopt the approach that William James called "radical empiricism" and the Dalai Lama has called "first-person empiricism" (pp. 27-29).

At the same time, it is incumbent upon those who, frustrated at the blockage of public access to these unusual and highly productive methods, are participating in autonomous underground experiential studies, inform themselves thoroughly of the possible medical and psychological complications and be appropriately prepared.

Finally, it is important to remember that with this, as with other so-called entheogenic medicines, the spiritual, mystical and cosmic dimensions of existence, which *the substances do not create but reveal* – are acknowledged with respect and humility.

References

Davis, Wade & Weil, Andrew T. "Identity of a New World Psychoactive Toad" in: *Ancient Mesoamerica*, 3 (1992), 51-59.

Grof, Stanislav. *When the Impossible Happens*. Boulder, CO: Sounds True, Inc. 2006.

Grof, Stanislav and Grof, Christina. *Holotropic Breathwork*. Albany, NY: State University of New York Press, 2010.

Leary, Timothy, Metzner, Ralph & Alpert, Richard. *The Psychedelic Experience – A Manual based on the Tibetan Book of the Dead*. New Hyde Park, N.Y.: University Books, 1964.

Linn, S. F., Emerson, W., Linn, D., & Linn, M., *Remembering Our Home - Healing Hurts & Receiving Gifts From Conception to Birth*. Mahwah, NJ: Paulist Press, 1999.

Masters, Robert A. *Darkness Shining Wild: An Odyssey to the Heart of Hell & Beyond*. Temenos Press, 2005.

McKenna, Dennis. *The Brotherhood of the Screaming Abyss – My Life with Terence McKenna*. St. Cloud, MN: North Star Press, 2012.

McKenna, Terence & McKenna, Dennis. *The Invisible Landscape*. New York: Seabury Press, 1975.

Metzner, Ralph. *Alchemical Divination*. Berkeley, CA: Regent Press & Green Earth Foundation, 2009.

Metzner, Ralph. *MindSpace and TimeStream*. Berkeley, CA: Regent Press & Green Earth Foundation, 2009.

Metzner, Ralph. *The Life Cycle of the Human Soul*. Berkely, CA: Regent Press & Green Earth Foundation, 2011.

Metzner, Ralph. *Worlds Within and Worlds Beyond*. Berkeley, CA: Regent Press & Green Earth Foundation, 2013.

Narby, Jeremy. *The Cosmic Serpent – DNA and the Origins of Knowledge*. New York: J.P. Tarcher/Putnam, 1998.

Nichols, David E. "Hallucinogens." in: ***Pharmacology & Therapeutics, 101*** 131-181 (2004).

Oroc, James. *Tryptamine Palace – 5-MeO-DMT and the Sonoran Desert Toad*. Rochester, VT: Park Street Press, 2009.

Ott, Jonathan. *Shamanic Snuffs or Entheogenic Errhines*. Solothurn: Entheobotanica, 2001.

Schultes, Richard Evans and Hofmann, Albert. *Plants of the Gods*. New York: McGraw-Hill Book Co., 1979.

Shulgin, Alexander and Ann. *TIHKAL – The Continuation*, Berkeley, CA: Transform Press, 1997.

Strassman, Rick. *DMT: The Spirit Molecule*. Rochester, VT: Park Street Press, 2001.

Torres, Constantino Manuel & Repke, David B. *Anandenanthera – Visionary Plant of Ancient South America*. New York: Haworth Herbal Press, 2006.

Trachsel, Daniel. *Psychedelische Chemie*. Solothurn: Nachtschatten Verlag, 2000.

CD: *Spirit Soundings*, by Ralph Metzner & Kit Walker. Green Earth Foundation, 2012. (www.greenearthfound.org)

Printed in August 2021
by Rotomail Italia S.p.A., Vignate (MI) - Italy